Challenging Authority
How Ordinary People Change America

FRANCES FOX PIVEN

ROWMAN & LITTLEFIELD PUBLISHERS, INC.
Lanham • Boulder • New York • Toronto • Oxford

D0018432

ROWMAN & LITTLEFIELD PUBLISHERS, INC.

Published in the United States of America
by Rowman & Littlefield Publishers, Inc.
A wholly owned subsidiary of The Rowman & Littlefield Publishing Group, Inc.
4501 Forbes Boulevard, Suite 200, Lanham, Maryland 20706
www.rowmanlittlefield.com

Estover Road
Plymouth PL6 7PY
United Kingdom

Distributed by National Book Network

Copyright © 2006 by Frances Fox Piven
First paperback edition 2008

All rights reserved. No part of this publication may be reproduced,
stored in a retrieval system, or transmitted in any form or by any
means, electronic, mechanical, photocopying, recording, or otherwise,
without the prior permission of the publisher.

British Library Cataloguing in Publication Information Available

Library of Congress Cataloging-in-Publication Data

Piven, Frances Fox.
    Challenging authority : how ordinary people change America /
Frances Fox Piven.
        p. cm. — (Polemics)
    Includes index.
    1. Protest movements—United States—History. 2. United States—Politics and
government—History. 3. Elections—United States. 4. Civil disobedience—United States.
5. Political culture—United States. I. Title. II. Series.
    HN59.2.P557 2006
    322.40973—dc22   2006012517
    ISBN-13: 978-0-7425-1535-2 (cloth : alk. paper)
    ISBN-10: 0-7425-1535-4 (cloth : alk. paper)
    ISBN-13: 978-0-7425-6316-2 (pbk. : alk. paper)
    ISBN-10: 0-7425-6316-2 (pbk. : alk. paper)
    eISBN-13: 978-0-7425-6340-7
    eISBN-10: 0-7425-6340-5

⊗™ The paper used in this publication meets the minimum requirements of American
National Standard for Information Sciences—Permanence of Paper for Printed Library
Materials, ANSI/NISO Z39.48-1992.

Challenging Authority

POLEMICS

Stephen Eric Bronner, Series Editor

The books in the Polemics series confront readers with provocative ideas by major figures in the social sciences and humanities on a host of controversial issues and developments. The authors combine a sophisticated argument with a lively and engaging style, making the books interesting to even the most accomplished scholar and appealing to the general reader and student.

MEDIA WARS
News at a Time of Terror
By Danny Schechter

THE COLLAPSE OF LIBERALISM
Why America Needs a New Left
By Charles Noble

IMPERIAL DELUSIONS
American Militarism and Endless War
By Carl Boggs

MURDERING MYTHS
The Real Story Behind the Death Penalty
By Judith Kay

PRIMETIME POLITICS
The Truth about Conservative Lies, Corporate Control, and Television Culture
By Philip Green

GAY MARRIAGE AND DEMOCRACY
Equality for All
By R. Claire Snyder

CHALLENGING AUTHORITY
How Ordinary People Change America
By Frances Fox Piven

Contents

CHAPTER

ONE

❦

Introduction

A little patience, and we shall see the reign of witches pass over, their spells dissolve, and the people, recovering their true sight, restore their government to its true principals. It is true that in the meantime we are suffering deeply in spirit, and incurring the horrors of a war and long oppressions of enormous public debt. . . . If the game runs sometimes against us at home we must have patience til luck turns, and then we shall have an opportunity of winning back the principles we have lost, for this is a game where principles are at stake.

— THOMAS JEFFERSON, from a letter he sent
in 1798 after the passage of the Sedition Act

T HIS BOOK argues that ordinary people exercise power in American politics mainly at those extraordinary moments when they rise up in anger and hope, defy the rules that ordinarily govern their daily lives, and, by doing so, disrupt the workings of the institutions in which they are enmeshed. The drama of such events, combined with the disorder that results, propels new issues to the center of political debate, issues that were previously suppressed by the managers of political parties that depend on welding together majorities. When the new issues fracture or threaten to fracture electoral coalitions, political leaders try to restore order and stem voter defections by proffering reforms. These are the conditions that produce the democratic moments in American political development.

Admittedly, this is not the usual wisdom. Indeed, almost all of what we are taught about the workings of the American political system argues that the normal procedures of our electoral-representative institutions can be made to work for people lower down in the social order, if only they organize, if only they exert themselves to make their grievances known, and if only they try harder. In this book I will show that it is in fact precisely at the moments when people act outside of electoral norms that electoral-representative procedures are more likely to realize their democratic potential.

Most people equate electoral participation with democracy, with the deep and compelling belief that the people rule by participating in elections. Across the globe and throughout modern history, people have risked their lives for this idea—and no wonder. It implies that the holders of state power ultimately depend on the approval of ordinary people. This is an amazing possibility. Policies determining war or peace; that shape the location and pace of economic development and therefore the fate of local communities; and that even influence (when they do not determine) the availability of the resources that make possible human life itself, from the air we breath, to the water we drink, to medical care, to the pension or welfare check that pays for food and shelter—all are presumably subject to the approval of the mass public, of the voters who decide who will occupy positions of state authority.

This is another way of saying that democracy rests on the existence of electoral-representative arrangements. If most citizens are entitled to vote in periodic elections for the persons who will hold state office, and if they can communicate freely and associate freely, then those government officials will be bound to take citizen preferences into account in their crucial, life-shaping decisions.[1]

In the real American political world, there are numerous obstacles to the realization of this ideal. Some have to do simply with the unequal distribution of the franchise. When some voters carry more weight in the election of state authorities than other voters, the democratic ideal is compromised. In the United States, voters in less populous states have much more weight than voters in populous states in the election of senators and presidential electors, for example. Historically, southern and rural voters also had more weight in the election of representatives to the House, both as a result of the three-fifths rule, which I will discuss later, and as a result of the drawing of congressional district lines to underrepresent urban areas.[2]

Then there is the impediment of a web of rules and procedures governing access to the vote itself, with the result that large numbers of ostensibly eligible voters, especially lower income voters, are effectively disenfranchised even today, the Voting Rights Act and the National Voter Registration Act notwithstanding. The result is the exclusion, by voter disqualification and procedural encumbrances, of groups described by Richard McCormick as the "discordant social elements" who are the potential constituents of third-party efforts, or simply the likely supporters of the existing party opposition.[3] McCormick was writing about the nineteenth century when literacy tests, poll taxes, and onerous voter registration procedures were introduced to inhibit voting by blacks and poor whites in the South, and by the immigrant working class in the North. Literacy tests and poll taxes are a thing of the past. Nevertheless, an array of other strategies, from intimidation to misinformation to vote stealing, are still available and still used, as the charges of fraud in the conduct of the presidential elections of 2000 and 2004 suggest.

Other longstanding limits on democratic influence include the walling off of crucial parts of government from exposure to the electorate. In American history, a powerful appointed federal judiciary has played a large role in undercutting the decisions of elected representatives. Similarly, our central bank, which Kevin Phillips defines as our principal wealth-creating institution, is shielded from electoral influence.[4] And so is the ever-growing bureaucracy on all levels of government insulated from electoral politics, by the terms of the appointment of its officials, by bureaucratic organizational barriers, and by the sheer technical opacity of bureaucratic procedures.

Still, many officials, including those who appoint the federal judiciary, the governors of the Federal Reserve, and the top levels of our bureaucracies, must stand for election. Democracy, says Schumpeter, is "that institutional arrangement for arriving at political decisions in which individuals acquire the power to decide by means of a competitive struggle for the people's vote."[5] In other words, periodic elections for state office will make candidates accountable to mass publics. That hope in turn depends crucially on the activities of political parties.

"The classical definition of democracy," said the noted political scientist E. E. Schattschneider, "left a great, unexplored breach in the theory of modern government, the zone between the sovereign people and the government which is the habitat of the parties."[6] The political parties make electoral-representative arrangements democratically effective, when they are effective, because they aggregate otherwise atomized voters around coherent political alternatives. Without parties, voters are merely unconnected individuals, typically distracted and indifferent to affairs of state, their preferences easily trumped by any organized cabal. And voters without parties are incapable of scrutinizing and assessing a labyrinthine system of government and the complex and arcane policies it produces, with the consequence that organized interests operate virtually unimpeded. Only parties are capable of welding voters into an effective force to which the holders of state office must respond. And only parties can hold remote office holders accountable to the mandate of the voters.

In democratic principle, parties seeking to win office in an electoral-representative system exert themselves to listen to voter opinion, searching out and articulating voter preferences in picking their slate and fashioning their symbols and programmatic appeals. Then they work to mobilize their likely voters around programs and candidates, and to bring them to the polls. Once in power, the winning party looks ahead to the next election and tries to hold its representatives accountable to the voters who elected them by translating campaign promises into public policies. Political parties, in other words, organize otherwise dispersed voters around political alternatives and then discipline elected officials to pursue those alternatives. They are the agencies that actualize—or fail to actualize—the ideal of reciprocity between voters and state elites on which the democratic idea rests.

Actual political parties have always fallen short, and American parties have fallen far short. The catalogue of reasons is long, and mostly familiar. The democratic idea posits a world in which the vote is the sole currency of power. Unlike other resources for influence, such as wealth or arms, the vote can in principle be widely and equally distributed. And viewed abstractly, electoral-representative arrangements are indeed a remarkable institutional construction. Think of it: a new resource is created and widely and equally distributed, and in principle that equal resource overrides all of the inequalities of social life in the selection of state leaders.

In the real world, however, these inequalities are translated into currencies that penetrate electoral spheres and distort the fundamental interdependence between equal voters and state leaders on which the democratic idea depends. Thus contemporary critiques of American politics rightly emphasize the corrupting influence of money, which makes politicians seeking election at least as beholden to the business contributors who pay for their campaigns as to the voters whom these campaigns are intended to persuade. And with the rise of television as the main medium of campaigning, not only does the capacity for voter manipulation grow, but so does the need for contributions, and therefore the influence of big money. Because money buys the means to reach and persuade voters, money buys votes today as surely as once did the two-dollar bribe.

Then there is the distortion of incumbency that results from the multiple ways that the prerogatives of office can be used to influence elections. For one thing, incumbency grants contenders visibility and a platform. And, because incumbents trade their influence on policy for campaign contributions, it is nearly impossible to defeat incumbent members of Congress.

The American two-party system also inhibits coherent and responsible party appeals and governance, for the simple reason that each party in its drive to win a majority works to paper over or ignore fractious divisions that would make a voting majority unlikely.[7] The institutional reasons for restriction of electoral contests to the two major parties have been much discussed. They include the legal arrangements, embedded in the Constitution and in state laws, which lead to single-member districts and plurality elections where only the candidate with the most votes wins office, thus excluding the candidates of minorities from any representative role. Moreover, over time, the major parties have colluded in the development of an array of additional legal obstructions to ward off pesky challengers, including absurdly difficult procedures for ballot access.

The two-party system has been praised for its ability to reduce political fractiousness and extremism, at least during elections campaigns. This is the much-admired "big tent" effect, which both Republicans and Democrats alike claim to endorse. But while the big-tent party may succeed in muffling conflict, it also has deeply undemocratic effects. When party leaders and their candidates require broad majorities to win public office, they try to hold the allegiance of the diverse groups that a majority must include by avoiding issues that will generate conflict. Instead, they search for the consensual appeals, and especially the consensual symbols, that will preserve and enlarge their voter coalitions. In a large and diverse country, with sharp inequalities of condition and divergent cultural aspirations, this inevitably means avoiding the issues that speak to the interests and symbols important to some blocs of voters for fear of antagonizing other blocs of voters. Hence candidates are inclined to campaign on largely uncontroversial symbols of family or flag or freedom.

These long-standing distortions in American democratic arrangements have always been with us. But they are periodically overridden by popular uprisings, and then, when the uprisings recede, so do the democratic currents they have unleashed. American politics returns to its default position where special influences, especially business influences, matter most, and the public arenas created by democratic institutions become arenas for popular manipulation. Our own era offers a vivid example.

Over the past three decades, business domination of politics has become nearly total. The flood of money into electoral campaigns overwhelms the influence of voter preferences, if only because money is used to subvert the reasoned judgment of voters with mass advertising. So arrogant have the Republicans become as the favored political party of business, that their new "K Street strategy" threatens to punish lobbyists who also contribute to the opposition party, which is of course traditional business practice.[8] The eighteenth-century doctrine of the separation of state and market is invoked to discredit government initiatives that shield ordinary people from economic or environmental harm even while whatever separation existed between government and powerful market actors disappears.[9] Corporations open Washington offices, launch political action committees, flood electoral campaigns with contributions, and beef up the trade associations that are now virtually a branch of government. Corporate lobbyists intrude into the inner workings of government, and politicians leave office to morph into business executives, while other business executives morph into politicians. The result is to convert public programs into private political spoils.[10]

Democratic deliberation in a large and modern society depends on the media to inform the citizenry about their political world. In the United States, the information and interpretation that voters require for democratic participation is hostage to a mass media under increasingly consolidated corporate control. Relatively little deeply controversial news is likely to make its way onto the main airwaves or into print. The Downing Street memos, which reported Pentagon planning for an invasion of Iraq was far advanced by the summer of 2002, and which also described White House efforts to doctor the intelligence and facts to justify the invasion, were ignored on the editorial pages of four of the five major U.S. newspapers.[11] While the mainstream media falls under the control of corporate allies of the administration, the far right continues to expand its print and cable television outlets.[12] It uses these outlets to launch coordinated campaigns to harass and intimidate mainstream journalists as "liberal" or unpatriotic if they deviate from the administration line. The administration, together with its allies in the organized right has also trained its sights on the public broadcasting networks, "stocking the corporation with G.O.P. loyalists," in the words of the *New York Times*, and threatening public broadcasting with big budget cuts.[13] "[F]evered agents of an angry ideology," said Bill Moyers, "wage war on all things public, including public broadcasting."[14]

Democratic deliberation is also stymied by the contemporary pattern of deception by government officials. Presumably voters choose the party and the candidate whose record and promises come closest to matching their own preferences. But Orwellian uses of rhetoric would seem to rule out such deliberation on the part of citizen voters.

Candidate George W. Bush campaigned in 2000 as a "compassionate conservative" but as president he offered a budget that slashed monies for school lunches, child care, and after-school programs. And President Bush on the campaign trail in 2004 asserted that most of his tax cuts went to low- and middle-income Americans. In fact, 53 percent will go to people with incomes in the top 10 percent.[15] Half of all taxpayers received a cut of less than $100 in the first year, and by 2005 three-quarters will get less than $100, while the wealthiest 1 percent will get an average tax reduction of nearly $100,000 a year.[16]

The Medicare Prescription Drug Act passed in 2003 was advertised by the president as the fulfillment of his campaign pledge to provide drug benefits for seniors. The drug benefits are limited and patchy, but the legislation includes very large subsidies to the pharmaceutical companies, as well as legislated protection to the companies against competition from drug imports. To get the measure through Congress, the administration understated its true costs by more than $300 billion, and even threatened to fire a Medicare actuary if he shared his estimates with Congress.[17]

And Candidate Bush told voters in campaign 2000 that in foreign policy, "If we're an arrogant nation, [the people of the world] will resent us. If we're a humble nation but strong, they'll welcome us." This commitment did not restrain the administration's strategy of "preemptive" war in Iraq, which threatened to wreck an international system of multilateral alliances. And the buildup to war led to more egregious public deception, including repeated claims that Iraq had stockpiled "weapons of mass destruction," and that Iraq had supported Al Qaeda, claims that were not substantiated by U.S. intelligence. It is no longer outlandish to wonder whether the fear and excitement of the war against terror and the war against Iraq were at least in part electoral strategies to build support for the regime—distracting the public from the uncertainties and troubles of a weak economy with the fear and excitement of war and nationalist enthusiasms—so far with considerable success, at least in the elections of 2002 and 2004.

And then there is the readiness with which public officials have come to scorn the norms that make electoral-representative arrangements at least partially effective in holding officials accountable to voters.

Consider some examples. One is the problem of fraud in the conduct of elections. Election fraud is obviously not new, but the scale and license with which it is undertaken may be extreme, as the debacle over the Florida vote in election 2000 and the ensuing appointment of the president by the Supreme Court suggested. The problem reemerged in election 2004, particularly in a number of battleground states where ostensibly neutral election officials were closely tied to the Republican Party.

Another sort of reckless manipulation for partisan advantage was evident in the practice of arbitrary redistricting. Defying long-established tradition that congressional district lines are to be redrawn once a decade, Republican legislatures in Colorado and Texas chose to redraw district lines that had only recently been adopted, fashioning odd district shapes that would increase their advantage. When Democratic legislators in Texas fled the state in an effort to prevent a quorum vote on the new lines, not only the Texas state police but the Federal Department of Homeland Security were summoned to make them return.[18]

Or think of the revelations about the uses of federal program budgets for partisan advertising, as when Medicare funds were used to produce video "news releases" for television, with prepackaged news segments and actors posing as journalists talking about the marvels of the president's prescription drug program for seniors. Or consider how journalist Armstrong Williams was paid $240,000 to plug the president's No Child Left Behind Act, while syndicated columnist Maggie Gallagher received a $21,500 contract from the Department of Health and Human Services to promote the Bush marriage promotion initiative.[19]

The success thus far of this political manipulation is owed in large part to the fact that a politicized business class has assiduously cultivated right-wing populist allies, especially the Christian Right and gun enthusiasts, who contribute popular support and legitimacy to a business-dominated regime. The alliance of business and religious populism is in turn bound together by a newly hegemonic doctrine that regards the operation of market forces as the workings of a divine providence and treats government measures that moderate market processes as moral trespass. Or rather, the doctrine is new to our time, since it blends together centuries-old ideas about laissez-faire with a centuries-old

Protestant yearning for salvation. Christian fundamentalism is joined to market fundamentalism, justifying, as Fred Block summarizes, "a systematic effort to . . . reduce the role of government, lower taxes, restore the central role of religion and piety in public life . . . [so as to] make it possible for us to recapture our greatness as a people."[20]

In short, the United States looks more and more like the authoritarian populist regimes that have been dominant in Latin America and Southeast Asia. Colin Crouch's description of what he calls "post-democracy" is apt:

> [W]hile elections still exist . . . public electoral debate is a tightly controlled spectacle, managed by rival teams of professionals expert in the techniques of persuasion, and considering a small range of issues selected by those teams. The mass of citizens plays a passive, quiescent, even apathetic part, responding only to the signals given them. Behind this spectacle of the electoral game politics is really shaped in private by interaction between elected governments and elites which overwhelmingly represent business interests.[21]

Some voters turn to religion. Many others simply become more cynical. Indeed, political cynicism has been rising for four decades, as voter participation has declined. To be sure, these trends were interrupted by the rally and excitement generated by the wars on terror and Iraq, as they were earlier briefly interrupted by the demagogic appeals of Ronald Reagan. Nevertheless, the longer-term decline seems inexorable. In 1964 about three-fourths of the American public said they trusted Washington most or all of the time. By the mid-1990s, the percentage trusting the national government had fallen below 20 percent.[22] Rosenstone and Hansen sum up the data:

> Between the 1960s and the 1980s, more and more citizens came to believe that politics and government were so complicated that ordinary people could not understand them; internal efficacy fell. Likewise, more and more citizens came to doubt that public officials cared about the views of the people, and came to wonder whether they had any say in what the government did; external efficacy fell.[23]

By the 1990s, the Gallup Organization reported that only 19 percent of those polled trusted Washington all or most of the time, and a majority thought that the federal government was really controlled by lobbyists.[24]

Meanwhile, Putnam calculated that the proportion of the public who reported working for a political party had declined from 6 percent in the early 1970s to just 3 percent in the mid-1990s.[25] The problem is not cynicism alone. Notwithstanding the extraordinary mobilization of volunteers and new voters in the tightly contested election of 2004, the parties and the campaign organizations are less likely to involve people. "The failure of political leaders and institutions to solicit, support, and encourage political participation accounted for over half the decline in work for political parties and almost two-thirds of the decline in contributions to political campaigns."[26] Over the longer term, the trend in declining voter turnout is likely to continue.[27]

Half a century ago, in the aftermath of World War II and the defeat of fascism, most political scientists viewed the American democracy with a self-satisfied complacency. It was not that our electoral-representative arrangements were without flaws. Rather they were simply the best that was possible. Thus Robert Dahl and Charles Lindblom argued in a much-admired book that the American political-economic order approximated democracy—they called the approximation polyarchy—in a less-than-perfect world.[28]

Only a little more than two decades later, perhaps jarred by the protest movements of the 1960s, Dahl and Lindblom were less sanguine:

> [W]ealth and income, along with many values that tend to cluster with wealth and income, such as education, status, and access to organizations, all constitute resources that can be used in order to gain influence over other people. Inequalities with respect to these matters are therefore equivalent to inequalities in access to political resources. . . . More concretely, the present distribution of resources in the United States presents a major obstacle to a satisfactory approximation of the goal of political equality. . . . And if certain options like voting, free speech, and due process have to be established as

"rights" to make democracy work, so also does a fairer share of income and wealth have to become a "right."[29]

Even more recently, Robert Dahl, writing about American constitutional arrangements and democracy, pronounced our political system to be "among the most opaque, complex, confusing, and difficult to understand," and goes on to show how badly the United States does when ranked against other established democracies on measures such as foreign aid, rates of incarceration, social expenditures, economic growth, and the ratio of poor to rich.[30]

Obviously, the inequalities of wealth and income that Dahl and Lindblom think are important to democracy are extreme in the United States, and are rapidly becoming more extreme.[31] Extreme inequality aggravates the pernicious problem of politicians for hire, simply because excesses of wealth are available for the bribery that can lead to the policies that produce more wealth. It is also the case that diverse forms of political participation among the citizenry are empirically correlated with income: the better-off vote more, join organizations more, communicate with their representatives more, and so on.[32]

Moreover, inequality is pernicious for other reasons that are well articulated in an American intellectual tradition that goes back to the revolutionary era. Extremes of inequality breed patterns of domination and subservience in the multiple social relations of everyday life, and these cultural patterns undermine democratic capabilities.[33] People who are rich come to expect not only their wealth, but also the multiple forms of entitlement, including the deference of others, that come with wealth. People who are very poor are not only materially deprived, but their circumstances can cost them respect and self-respect. Meanwhile, the affluent and the very affluent wall themselves off from the larger community in gated communities and private schools and services. Inequality, in other words, not only means that some have more influence than others. It also means that democratic values are pervasively undermined in the interactions of everyday life.[34]

Extremes of inequality are also associated with rising religiosity as people turn heavenward for the solution of the problems of daily life.[35] This is a familiar phenomenon. Elsewhere in the world, we associate growing inequality with an apocalyptic and fundamentalist politics. In the United States, increasing inequality not only reflects the policy successes of the organized right, but so far at least it has helped fuel the growth of the populist right. People turn to God and God's law for solace, and they turn to fundamentalist megachurches for the services that government once provided. And, just to be sure, the current administration is directing government funds to many of these churches, presumably to provide social services, but more likely to build bastions of the right-wing machine, especially in the African American and Hispanic communities that have thus far resisted its blandishments.

Nor are we strong with regard to other conditions that Dahl and Lindblom think fosters democracy, including a society in which business does not have a privileged position, where a shared culture is binding on the ruling class, and one that is open to change and is not doctrinaire with regard to private ownership. None of these conditions can reasonably be said to prevail in the United States at the beginning of the twenty-first century.

Others offer an even stronger critique. In 1969, just a few years before Dahl and Lindblom issued their dour reassessment of American democratic prospects, Sheldon Wolin described our maladies as including "the decay of the cities, the increasing cultural and economic gap between our minorities and our majority, crisis in the educational system, destruction of our natural environment—which call for the most precedent-shattering and radical measures."[36] Successive generations of critics have become grimmer still. In 1983, Josh Cohen and Joel Rogers opened a book titled *On Democracy* with the words "These are dark times" and went on to list problems very much like the list I offered earlier, including a massive business political offensive, cutbacks in social spending and environmental destruction, low levels of political participation, and so on.[37] Kevin Phillips talks of the "influx of lawyers, corporate representatives, and trade associations" that turned Washington into "the leading interest-group bazaar of the Western World."[38] Or Paul Krugman, writing in the *New York Times* in June of 2003, concludes a column on the conduct of the Bush administration by suggesting that "our political system has become utterly, and perhaps irrevocably, corrupted."[39]

Usually when this sort of evidence of the malfunctioning of American electoral-representative arrangements is reviewed, it is to imply that it was once, in some unspecified rosy past, better. In fact, democracy, understood as a specific set of institutional arrangements allowing the population a voice in government, has never worked well in the United States. When exactly was the golden age when electoral-representative arrangements did function, if not perfectly, at least to create something like a democratic polity? Certainly not in the nineteenth century, no matter that it is often depicted as an era of democratic exuberance. To be sure, in the early decades of that century the franchise was successively extended until nearly all white men enjoyed the right to vote, and popular politics at the time is typically characterized as tumultuous and vibrant, as a kind of golden age of democratic politics.[40] Parades and picnics and high voter turnout notwithstanding, political participation for most of the nineteenth century was stamped and molded by intense religious and ethnic allegiances, and this political culture was in turn cultivated by political parties steeped in patronage, at the national, state, and local levels. Voters were organized by armies of foot soldiers, to be sure, but the foot soldiers were on a payroll. The significance of these arrangements was that voter participation was organized in terms of ethno-cultural identities and personal favors, thus largely walling off voters from influence on the big and potentially divisive policies of the day, including currency, tariff, and the internal infrastructure developments that were decisively shaping the American political-economic order.

Meanwhile, this was also the era when corporate and especially railroad power grew and came to dominate national, state, and local governments. Corporations secured favorable action on tariffs, obtained huge land giveaways and subsidies, commandeered government agencies to do railroad work, and then used the further wealth thus accrued to tighten their grip not only on state governments but also on the national government. Control of state legislatures guaranteed control of the Senate, and control of the Senate yielded control of the U.S. Supreme Court. Boies Penrose, a late-nineteenth-century Republican senator from Pennsylvania, captured the dynamic in a speech to a business audience: "I believe in a division of labor. You send us to Congress;

we pass the laws under which you make money . . . and you further contribute to our campaign funds to pass more laws to enable you to make more money."[41] James B. Weaver, the People's Party of America presidential nominee in 1892, summed it up: Plutocracy "has usurped the Government . . . filled the Senate . . ., controls the popular branch of the legislature, and it has not hesitated to tamper with our Court of last resort."[42] The party's platform was more eloquent:

> [W]e meet in the midst of a nation brought to the verge of moral, political, and material ruin. Corruption dominates the ballot-box, the legislatures, the Congress, and touches even the ermine of the bench. The people are demoralized; most of the States have been compelled to isolate the voters at the polling places to prevent universal intimidation or bribery. The newspapers are largely subsidized or muzzled, public opinion silenced, business prostrated, our homes covered with mortgages, labor impoverished, and the land concentrating in the hands of capitalists. The urban workmen are denied the right of organization for self protection. . . . Imported pauperized labor beats down their wages. . . .The fruits of the toil of millions are boldly stolen to build up colossal fortunes for a few.[43]

Or consider Elizabeth Sanders' summary of the uses of government by employers to defeat labor during this period. The Sherman Act of 1890, initially justified as a restraint on business monopoly, was turned into an anti-labor weapon by the judiciary.

> Federal judges (including William Howard Taft) discovered that although the Interstate Commerce Act intended no strict regulation of railroads, it could be used to punish railroad strikers or boycotters. In 1894, Cleveland's attorney general secured sweeping injunctions against the officers of the American Railway Union for obstructing rail traffic duing the Pullman strike. Eugene V. Debs and other strike leaders were found guilty of contempt for violating an injunction, and a federal circuit judge in Chicago ruled that the rail workers' actions fell under the Sherman Act's prohibitions, as a "conspiracy against travel and transportation by railroad."[44]

Money corruption, in other words, is also not new. Overlacker's 1932 study of campaign financing found that almost 70 percent of the contributions to the 1928 federal election campaigns were in donations of over $1,000.[45] As Michael Tomasky recently pointed out, the rise of the New Deal did not change the pattern. Franklin Delano Roosevelt's campaigns were financed by business and later by unions; John F. Kennedy campaigned in the 1960 primary in West Virginia by purportedly lining the pockets of local sheriffs; and in succeeding years, oilmen regularly and openly passed fat envelopes of cash to congressmen of both parties.[46] Even the level of deception is not new, as anyone who can remember the Watergate scandals will know.

The normal routes created by electoral-representative institutions provide at best a twisted and obstacle-strewn path for popular influence, when they provide any path at all. But there have nevertheless been periods of egalitarian reform in American political history. In the chapters that follow, I will analyze these episodes to show the crucial role of protest movements, and I will try to unravel the political dynamics through which movements came for a time to exercise some considerable influence on American politics, if only temporarily.

I begin this unraveling in the next chapter by turning to the theoretical question of why the ordinary people who band together in protest movements sometimes succeed in forcing concessions from their rulers. Merely to ask this question is to cast doubt on our usual assumption that power inevitably flows to those who have more of the things and attributes valued in social life. To be sure, usually it does. But there are also the historical occasions in which workers or peasants or rioters exercise power. In chapter 2, I discuss the distinctive kind of *disruptive* or *interdependent* power exercised by protest movements, and the conditions under which it can be actualized.

In chapter 3, I turn to my first case, the mobilization of disruptive power from below during events surrounding the American Revolution. At the time, electoral-representative arrangements were fragmented and incomplete, but popular power was nevertheless important in colonial and revolutionary America, and it typically took the form of the elemental physical threat wielded by "the people out-of-doors," or, more simply, the mob. The support of the mob not only made victory in the revolution possible, but the disruptive threat of the mob laid down some of the conditions for the establishment of a new nation. The "people out-of-doors" were not blind, but were moved by the promises of radical democracy. Their continuing threat power forced the founders to incorporate some elements of electoral democracy into the new constitutions of the states and the national government. Thus, in the tumult of the postrevolutionary period, American elites reluctantly constructed the building blocks of electoral-representative institutions. However inadequate measured against the principles of democracy, these arrangements did sometimes moderate the raw power of business and state elites. Moreover, they became the institutional context that determined the fate of subsequent protest movements.

I turn next in chapter 4 to the abolitionist movement. The abolitionist protests emerged in the context of developed electoral-representative arrangements, and at a time when the American party system had matured. The movement provides a striking illustration of the interplay of disruptive power and electoral politics. After decades of turmoil incited by the movement, culminating in the rupture of the existing party system and civil war, Lincoln declared the slaves emancipated, the constitution was amended to seal the victory, and the reconstruction of the South was attempted. These accomplishments were owed not to disruptive power alone, but to the impact of disruptive power on electoral politics.

Next, in chapter 5, I turn to the movements that prompted the major reforms of the twentieth century. The Great Depression saw an explosion of measures to regulate business, as well as labor and social welfare legislation. In the 1960s, the black freedom movement made major gains in dismantling the American apartheid system, and also forced the expansion and elaboration of New Deal reforms to new groups and new areas, including the introduction of governmental health insurance, and workplace and environmental regulation. In this chapter, I will not only analyze the dynamics of disruptive power and its impact on electoral politics, but I will also argue that dominant political interpretations of these twentieth-century developments, by ignoring protest movements, ultimately fail as explanations.

Finally, in chapter 6, I reverse the logic of my earlier analyses to examine the periods between episodes of major disruptive protest. I show that in each case, once protest subsides, few new egalitarian reforms are initiated. Moreover, the reforms won earlier are often whittled away. Dahl and Lindblom refer somewhat mysteriously to "rare intervals of crisis," as the occasions on which "nonincremental" reform may be won, but they quickly pass over these rare intervals to discuss the slow but steady workings of what they call incremental reform. I argue in chapter 6 that the slow and steady workings of normal politics are more likely to wear away the reforms won during those moments of crisis than they are to enlarge upon them.

In sum, the central question of this book is, given the power inequalities of American life and the extent to which electoral-representative arrangements are twisted by those inequalities, how does egalitarian reform ever occur in the United States? The rare intervals of nonincremental democratic reforms are responses to the rise of disruptive protest movements, and the distinctive kind of power that these movements wield. These movements are played out in the context of electoral-representative arrangements, and the interplay between the unfolding movement and electoral responses is important both in shaping the movement and in shaping responses to it. For now, however, I want to make the point that democratic successes flow not from the influence of voters and parties taken by themselves, but from the mobilization of a more fundamental kind of power that is rooted in the very nature of society, in the networks of social interdependence or cooperation that society implies. I call this disruptive power, and it is to a discussion of this kind of power that I now turn.

CHAPTER TWO

The Nature of
Disruptive Power

PUT ASIDE for the moment the dictates about power that are associated with electoral-representative institutions. When we consider
power abstractly, apart from particular institutional arrangements,
we usually assume it is rooted in the control of resources, especially
in control of wealth and force, or in the institutional positions that yield
control over wealth and force. This view is surely consistent with much
of our historical experience. The big landowner has power over small
peasants, the media mogul over vast publics, the rich over the poor,
armed troops over civilians, and so on. Variants of this view have been
endlessly elaborated by theorists of power, with long lists of the assets
and positional advantages associated with wealth or force, as when
Randall Collins says, "Look for the material things that affect interaction: the physical places, the modes of communication, the supply of
weapons, devices for staging one's public impression, tools and goods.[1]
. . . The resources for conflict are complex," he concludes. C. Wright
Mills emphasizes the resources for power available to the occupants of
"top" institutional roles.[2] And Charles Tilly points to "the economist's
factors of production: land, labor, capital, perhaps technical expertise
as well."[3]

Clearly, one variant or another of the widely held thesis that power
is based on control of wealth and force explains a good deal of our
experience. But it does not explain all of our experience. If most of the
time landowners have power over sharecroppers, there are also the less

frequent times when they do not. Even apart from electoral-representative arrangements, history is dotted with those occasions when people without wealth or coercive resources did exercise power, at least some power, at least for a time. How are we to understand that power?

All societies organize social life through networks of specialized and interdependent activities, and the more complex the society, the more elaborate these interdependent relations. Networks of cooperation and interdependence inevitably give rise to contention, to conflict, as people bound together by social life try to use each other to further their often distinctive interests and outlooks. And the networks of interdependence that bind people together also generate widespread power capacities to act on these distinctive interests and outlooks. Agricultural workers depend on landowners, but landowners also depend on agricultural workers, just as industrial capitalists depend on workers, the prince depends in some measure on the urban crowd, merchants depend on customers, husbands depend on wives, masters depend on slaves,[4] landlords depend on tenants, and governing elites in the modern state depend on the acquiescence if not the approval of enfranchised publics.

Unlike wealth and force, which are concentrated at the top of social hierarchies, the leverage inherent in interdependencies is potentially widespread, especially in a densely interconnected society where the division of labor is far advanced. This leverage can in principle be activated by all parties to social relations, and it can also be activated from below, by the withdrawal of contributions to social cooperation by people at the lower end of hierarchical social relations.

I call the activation of interdependent power *disruption*, and I think protest movements are significant because they mobilize disruptive power.[5] A movement, says Alberto Melucci, pushes conflict "beyond the limits of compatibility with the system in question, i.e. it breaks the rules of the game, puts forward non-negotiable objectives, questions the legitimacy of power."[6] What distinguishes movements in this sort of definition, says Ron Aminzade, "is a willingness to use unconventional, sometimes illegal or revolutionary, forms of collective action. . . . [S]ocial movements embrace disruptive actions rather than work within existing institutional frameworks."[7]

However, I use the term disruption here not merely to evoke unconventional, radical demands and tactics, but in a specific way to denote the leverage that results from the breakdown of institutionally regulated cooperation, as in strikes, whether workplace strikes where people withdraw their labor and shut down production or the provision of services, or student strikes where young people withdraw from the classroom and close down the university; or as in boycotts, whether by consumers who refuse to purchase goods and thus threaten profits, or by the women "hysterics" of the late nineteenth century who refused their role as sexual partners and service providers, or by farmers who refuse to bring their milk to market; or as in riots, where crowds break with the compact that usually governs civic life; or as in mass demands for relief or welfare, where people break with a pattern of cooperation based on norms of self-reliance and self-denial.

In other words, although agricultural laborers, industrial workers, the people in the urban crowd, are all at the bottom end of hierarchical relations—and are kept at the bottom by wealth and force and the ideologies, rules, and coercive threats that those with wealth and force deploy—they nevertheless all also have potential power. That power consists in their ability to disrupt a pattern of ongoing and institutionalized cooperation that depends on their continuing contributions. The great moments of equalizing reform in American political history have been responses to the threatened or actual exercise of this disruptive power. Of course, there are always multiple other influences on the shape of any major reform, but elite responses to large-scale disruption typically include measures that are at least to some degree intended to assuage the grievances that provoke people to defiance. In the United States, political representation in government, the end of chattel slavery, and the right to unionize and to social welfare protections, have all been won by the mobilization of disruptive power, or so I will argue.

Actual power relations are, of course, as tangled and intricate as social life itself. Urban, democratic, and capitalist societies generate multiple and crosscutting forms of interdependency—between husbands and wives, doctors and patients, students and teachers, beauticians and their clients, and so on. All of these relationships generate the potential for conflict and the exercise of power. And the exercise of power in one set of relations can work to dampen efforts to exercise power in another set of relations, as parents might succeed in dampening an inclination in their children for schoolroom rebellion, for example. All of this is complicated and interesting, and indeed it preoccupies some power analysts, particularly those identified with "exchange theory" who study the microdynamics of power among networks of individuals.[8]

I take for granted, however, that some relationships are much more important than others, and because they are, the threat or actuality of their disruption can yield both more substantial reforms to conciliate the disruptors, and more substantial efforts to suppress them. The dominant interdependencies, and the power contests they make possible, develop within economic relationships and within the political relationships that anchor state elites to the societies they rule. Thus the important interdependencies are rooted in the cooperative activities that generate the material bases for social life, and that sustain the force and authority of the state. When I speak of classes and class power, I mean the economic interdependencies between large aggregates of people bound together in relations of production and exchange and divided by the typically exploitative character of those relations. These economic relations are of course intertwined with political relations with the state—markets always depend on political authority—helping to explain both why state elites ordinarily buttress patterns of economic domination, and also why they sometimes intervene to modify them.[9]

Notice that this emphasis on the power capacities created by the interdependent relations that constitute society is broadly consistent with important theoretical traditions. It meshes with Norbert Elias's depiction of the development of European central states as propelled by the dynamics generated by the networks of interdependency of warrior societies.[10] It is consistent with the Marxist view that the power of the proletariat is created by the system of industrial capitalist relations in which workers are enmeshed. It fits Schumpeter's characterization of the capitalist state as the "tax state," which, because it depends on economic resources it does not control, ties state authorities in close interdependence with the owners of private property who do control those resources.[11] And this definition of power is also consistent with the democratic model of electoral-representative systems discussed in chapter 1 which in principle bind state authorities to the voting publics on whom they depend for election to office.

I need to comment on my use of the term "disruption." I use it here to describe a power strategy that rests on withdrawing cooperation in social relations. However, the word is widely used in the social movement literature to describe collective actions that are noisy, disorderly, or violent. A disruptive power strategy may be noisy, of course, and it may be disorderly or violent, but whether the withdrawal of cooperation takes these forms is entirely contingent. Let me explain.

Protest movements are usually associated with marches and rallies, with banners and shouts. I think this emphasis on what Michael Lipsky, in his 1970 study of the New York rent strike, called "showmanship" or "noise" results from an underlying conception of the protest movement as essentially a means of communication.[12] Lipsky made the case that the showmanship of the rent strikers was their main political resource because it activated reformers who then took up the grievances of the protesters. Leaving aside the specifics of the case—in fact, there was little significant reform produced by the efforts of these third parties— the protest movement consisted mainly of theater and press conferences that announced the bad housing conditions that justified rent strikes. However, while there were courtroom antics and the press coverage was good, there was very little actual rent striking.

Protest movements do try to communicate their grievances, of course, with slogans, banners, antics, rallies, marches, and so on. They do this partly to build the movement and its morale, and partly to appeal for allies. The reverberations of disruptive actions, the shutdowns or highway blockages or property destruction, are inevitably also communicative. But while disruption thus usually gives the protestors voice, voice alone does not give the protesters much power. To be sure, the authorities may try to muffle the voice of the protesters, restricting the size of rallies or marches, or where they gather or march. The reactions to disruption, however, are likely to be far more strident. In fact, the response of authorities to disruptive protests is frequently to profess to allow voice while preventing the disruption itself. Thus the picket line, originally a strategy to physically obstruct the scabs who interfered with the shutdown of production, has been turned by the courts into an informational activity, with requirements that limit the number of pickets, that specify that the picketers must keep moving, and so on.

Note, however, that the disruptive actions that I have named as examples may or may not be noisy, and may or may not entail violence. The generation of noise, as in the shouting and perhaps menacing behavior of the crowd, may be part of the mobilizing strategy of strikers or boycotters, but both strikes and boycotts can proceed quietly as well. John Adams wrote that on the night of the Boston Tea Party, "Boston was never more still and calm." The large crowd that had gathered at the wharf simply watched in silence as the chests of tea were broken open and dumped into the sea.[13] And when capitalists employ their disruptive power, by disinvesting from particular firms or industries or countries, for example, it can be done very quietly indeed.

The same goes for violence. Protest movements may or may not engage in violence against property or persons. Students of American social movements have been very timid about this issue. They tend to ignore episodes of violence that do occur, excluding them by fiat from their definition of social movements. I suspect they are influenced by their sympathy for recent social movements in the United States, particularly by the much-proclaimed "nonviolence" of the civil rights movement. After all, to claim that movements are characteristically nonviolent seems to give them the moral upper hand. They are also probably influenced by the much-cited conclusion of Charles, Louise, and Richard Tilly, writing about nineteenth-century European movements, that "[to] an important degree, the damage to objects and, especially, to persons *consisted* of elite reactions to the claims made by ordinary people: troops, police, and thugs acting under instructions from owners and officials attacked demonstrators, strikers, and squatters."[14] There is clearly some truth in this. Much of the violence associated with collective protest is the violence of authorities deploying force to restore normal institutional routines. Nevertheless, the Tillys overstated their case, and, more recently, Charles Tilly has conceded that violence plays a larger role in movements than he earlier claimed.[15]

The reiterated claim that protest movements are ordinarily nonviolent obfuscates more than it illuminates. To be sure, many forms of institutional disruption entail no violence on the part of the disruptors, at least at the outset. But both the claim to nonviolence and the practice of violence are questions of strategy, since both can be deployed in the effort to defend, and escalate, disruptive power. The claim to nonviolence serves the more obvious strategic purpose. Big Bill Haywood, well known as a one-time officer of the unruly and often violent Western Federation of Miners, was general organizer of the Industrial Workers of the World in 1912 when he led the Lawrence, Massachusetts, textile strike. Haywood was famous—and popular—as an orator who called for industrial sabotage and scoffed that he was "not a law-abiding citizen." Notwithstanding his inflammatory rhetoric, the strikes Haywood led were in fact not violent. The Lawrence textile strike was marked by it's extraordinary discipline, and during the strike of rubber workers a year later in Akron, Ohio, Haywood told the workers that there should be no violence, "not the destruction of one cent's worth of property, not one cross word."[16]

Violence by protesters is often treated as a purely moral issue, a stance that ignores the violence inherent in the institutional routines, such as the starvation wages paid to the Lawrence strikers, that are often the target of the protests. It also ignores the strategic uses of both violence and nonviolence by protest movements. Haywood, a veteran of the battles of the western miners, was no novice when it came to violence by strikers or by owners. His use of nonviolence was strategic. He was intent on avoiding the moral censure that violence would permit the factory owners to heap upon the strikers, moral censure that is typically used to excuse the violence of owners and the authorities.

Just as nonviolence can be strategic, so can violence be used strategically, and often defensively, to permit the disruptive action, the withdrawal of cooperation, to continue. Local activists in the South armed themselves to defend the nonviolent disruptions of the civil rights movement.[17] Similarly, striking workers may try to use physical threats to intimidate the scabs who threaten to replace them. In these instances, protesters turn to violence to defend their ability to withdraw contributions to interdependent relations.

Violence is not only used defensively. Gay Seidman shows the interplay between armed struggle and grassroots mobilization in the anti-apartheid movement in South Africa, for example.[18] Violent insurgency in Iraq has forced the American occupation to abandon much of its plan for the privatization of the Iraqi economy.[19] Closer to home, and whether intended or not, the riots, rat-packs and street muggings in the Harlem streets of the 1960s helped to defend that potentially valuable real estate from the gentrification that was even then being planned for the neighborhood. Now that the area has become safer, gentrification is proceeding apace.

My premise that power is rooted in patterns of specialization and the resulting social interdependencies suggests that power from below is there for the taking. If that were so, complex societies would reveal a drift toward equality. That, however, is too simple a conclusion. True, viewed abstractly, the capacity to disrupt ongoing economic, social, or political processes on which power rests is widely distributed, and increasingly so as societies become more complexly specialized and interrelated. But the ability to mobilize and deploy contributions to social cooperation in actual power contests varies widely and depends on specific and concrete historical circumstances. To appreciate this, we have to forego our tendency to speak in general terms of classes and systems. For some purposes, these abstractions are of course useful, but the interdependencies which sometimes make assertions of popular power possible don't exist in general or in the abstract. They exist for particular groups who are in particular relationships with particular capitalists or particular state authorities at particular places and particular times. Or, as Donald Kalb says, "We really have to embrace complexity." [20]

Strategies for the exercise of interdependent or disruptive power do not emerge automatically or inevitably from the existence of cooperative relations. To the contrary, cooperation and the interdependence it entails are ubiquitous; disruption and the effort to exercise power are not. The actualization of the power capacities inherent in interdependent relations is always conditional on the ability of the parties to the relationship to withhold or threaten to withhold their cooperation, and this capacity depends on other features of these relations beyond the fact of interdependence. Disruptive power is not actionable until a series of problems are solved.

First there is the problem of recognizing the fact of interdependence, and therefore the potential for power from below, in the face of ruling class definitions which privilege the contributions of dominant groups to social life, and may indeed even eradicate the contributions of lower status groups. Economic and political interdependencies are real in the sense that they have real ramifications in the material bases of social life and in the exercise of coercive force. But they are also cultural constructions. Thus the money contributions of husbands to family relations have always been given much more emphasis than the domestic services of wives, the contributions of entrepreneurial capital more weight than the productive labor of workers, and so on. Before people are likely to withdraw their contributions as a strategy for exercising power, they need to recognize the large part those contributions play in mating or production or political or religious relationships. In other words, this first step in the mobilization of interdependent power is itself contingent on how people understand the social relations in which they are enmeshed.

Second, the activation of disruptive power ordinarily requires that people break rules. This is a troubling assertion, so let me explain. If patterned cooperation is the stuff of social life, it is also not invented anew by the people who engage in it. Most cooperative relations are to a greater or lesser extent institutionalized. I mean by that that they are rule-governed. The rules governing behavior in cooperative activities are not neutral. To the extent that they are formed in the context of the power inequalities resulting from concentrations of wealth and force, rules work to suppress the actualization of the interdependent power inherent in social cooperation.

Of course, rules or norms are also the basic postulates of collective life. They order human activities, telling people how to till the fields or work their machines or mate or die. They make available to contemporaries the wisdom of accumulated experience, secure people against the totally unexpected in social encounters, and they make possible the tacit cooperation that is social life.

But if rules are basic to group life, so is the play of power, the effort to use others to achieve ends even against opposition. Inevitably, therefore, rules also become strategies for power, strategies by which some people try to make other people serve their will. Rules do this by specifying the behaviors that are permissible by different parties to interdependent relations. And since the rules are fashioned to reflect prevailing patterns of domination made possible by concentrated wealth, force, and institutional position, they typically prohibit some people but not other people from using the leverage yielded by social interdependence. Moreover, rules are not merely formal prescriptions but, as Sewell argues, are intertwined with deeper interpretations, with schemata or metaphors that explain and justify social life as it is.[21]

And once successfully promulgated, rules constitute a new exterior and constraining social reality. Rules establishing property rights give some people exclusive right to the use and disposal of valued material resources, thus anchoring the dependence of labor on capital in the first instance, and safeguarding the right of capital to use the leverage inherent in interdependence. By contrast, a long history of rules dating from medieval law has restricted the right of workers to withhold their labor; or forbidden them from forming "combinations," joining in boycotts, or turning to public relief to tide them over the suspension of cooperation; or as in the contemporary United States, the rules carefully specify the conditions under which workers can or cannot strike.

It follows that the rules themselves often become the focus of group and class contention, including the episodic exercise of disruptive power. Thus rules change over time, not only in response to new assertions of the power yielded by wealth and force, but also in response to mobilizations from below. As a result, while rules generally tend to inhibit the activation of disruptive power, some rules may also enable its use, or they at least may provide legitimacy and therefore some protection for the exercise of interdependent power from below.[22] Only consider how regularly social movements go into battle charging that the actions or policies they are protesting are wrong because they violate the rules prescribed by law or custom.

Nevertheless, a broad generalization emerges from these observations. Because cooperative social relations are institutionalized in ways that reflect reigning power inequalities, the actualization of interdependent power is often conditional on the ability of people to defy the rules and dominant interpretations governing social relations.

Third, contributions to ongoing economic and political activities are often made by many individuals, and these multiple contributions must be coordinated for the effective mobilization of disruptive power. Workers, villagers, parishioners, or consumers have to act in concert before the withdrawal of their contributions exerts a disruptive effect on the factory or the church or the merchant. This is the classical problem of solidarity, of organizing for joint action, that workers, voters, or community residents confront when they try to deploy their leverage over those who depend on them, for their labor, or their votes, or their acquiescence in the normal patterns of civic life.

As numerous analysts have argued, the social relations created by a stable institutional context may go far toward solving the coordination problem. When village social organization was relatively intact, Barrington Moore argued, it provided the solidarity that enabled people to act against the new impositions associated with the fall of the ancien régime.[23] E. P. Thompson made a similar point about the tight social organization of the English village, which was crucial first in the mounting of Luddite assaults on factories, and later in protecting the assailants from informants.[24] On the other hand, the importance of underlying social organization is often overstated.[25] Street mobs can mobilize quickly, taking advantage of public gatherings such as markets or hangings or simply crowded streets, and the participants may not know each other personally, although they are likely to be able to read the signs of group, class, or neighborhood identity that the crowd displays.

Fourth, as noted earlier, social life is complicated, and political action takes form within a matrix of social relations. Those who try to mobilize disruptive power must overcome the constraints typically imposed by their multiple relations with others, as when would-be peasant insurgents are constrained by the threat of religious excommunication, or when labor insurgents are constrained by family ties. English Methodist preachers invoked for their parishioners the awesome threat of everlasting punishment in hell that would be visited on Luddite insurgents in the early nineteenth century.

Conversely, however, multiple ties may facilitate disruptive power challenges.[26] The church that ordinarily preaches obedience to worldly authority may sometimes, for whatever reasons, encourage the rebels, as occurred during the course of the Solidarity movement in Poland, or during the civil rights movement in the United States. Wives and mothers who typically urge caution may become allies in the insurgency, as in the fabled film *Salt of the Earth*. Even state authorities may help to foment insurgency, as the lieutenant governor of Pennsylvania did when he told assembled steelworkers in Homestead in 1936 that steel was now open territory for union organizers and that they could count on government relief funds if they were to strike.[27] Later that summer, the governor himself told a Labor Day rally in Pittsburgh that never during his administration would state troops be used to break a strike, and "the skies returned the crowd's response."[28]

Fifth, when people attempt to exercise disruptive or "interdependent" power, they have to see ways of enduring the suspension of the cooperative relationship on which they also depend, and to withstand any reprisals they may incur. This is less evident for the participants in mobbing or rioting, whose action is usually short-lived, and who are likely to remain anonymous. But when workers strike, they need to feed their families and pay the rent, and consumer boycotters need to be able to get by for a time without the goods or services they are refusing to purchase.

Sixth and finally, people have to be able to withstand or face down the threat of exit that is typically provoked by disruption. Husbands confronting rebellious wives may threaten to walk out, employers confronting striking workers may threaten to relocate or to replace workers, and so on. Even rioters risk precipitating the exit of partners to cooperative relationships, as when small businesses fled from slum neighborhoods in the wake of the ghetto riots of the 1960s.

All of these conditions are simultaneously objective and subjective, material and cultural, and these dimensions are tightly bound together in a dialectical relationship. The reigning ideas of a particular time and place may suppress the importance of the contributions of people lower in the social hierarchy. But the real and material activities of daily life, of the work people do, of the services they provide, may nevertheless prompt them to recognize their interdependent power, and they are often helped to do so by persisting subcultures that celebrate resistance and victory. People can also overestimate their leverage, sometimes because they imagine that God or fate is on their side, but God and fate can disappoint, and their disruptive mobilization can be defeated. Rules are similarly cultural constructions, but they are backed up by sanctions that can be very objective and material. The ability to act in concert is in part a product of culture, or of common identities that organizers and activists try to construct, but common identities are also influenced by objective circumstances, and action on those identities can change objective circumstances. The matrix of multiple relations within which interdependent power is mobilized is similarly both interpretive and real, insofar as real consequences flow from the actions of the people involved in those relations. Obviously, the threat of exit can be just that, a threat that may or may not be acted upon. But it can also be very real. Some plant managers merely threaten to move to Mexico or Bangladesh. And a good many plant managers actually do.

Repertoires

Strategies to overcome the obstacles to the actualization of interdependent power are not solved anew with each challenge. Rather these strategies become embedded in memory and culture, in a language of resistance. They become a *repertoire*. I use the word to describe a historically specific constellation of strategies to actualize interdependent power. The term was introduced by Charles Tilly who defined it as the inventory of available means of collective action.[29] He restricted the term to forms of collective action deployed by ordinary people, while I think the term should be used more broadly to include elite strategies of contention.

All parties to contested relations need to solve the problems of actionability, including those at the top end of social relations. In fact, social and economic change ordinarily spurs the invention of new power strategies (or repertoires) by dominant groups before it prompts new initiatives from below. The reason is probably simply that ruling groups are ordinarily better positioned to take advantage of new conditions and to adapt their strategies of contestation. They are more likely to have the scope of information, the experts, and the communication networks to recognize changing interdependencies; they are less fearful of existing rules because they understand their ability to deploy wealth and force to evade or to change them; the problem of collective action is usually more easily solved; they ordinarily have the advantage in contests that require endurance; and so on.

Still, sooner or later the strategic advantage yielded to elites by exogenous change is countered by the development of new repertoires from below. Spurred by new hardships or new opportunities, people do in time discover the power capacities embedded in particular patterns of economic and/or political interdependency, in a process influenced over time both by the experience of previous struggles and by the reforms yielded by those earlier struggles. Gradually they develop interpretations that counter reigning ideologies that deny the importance of their contributions to new economic and political relations. And they develop the solidarities and networks that make possible the concerted action necessary for effective leverage within these relationships, or they politicize existing solidarities and networks.

The translation of institutional possibility into political action is also influence by this two-sided—or more accurately multisided—character of repertoires. Strategies are forged in a dance of conflict and cooperation between the parties to interdependent relations. The strategies of workers or tenants or students or peasants and the strategies of the employers or landlords or teachers or overlords with whom they contend are shaped in a "dialogic" interaction, and, indeed, in "multilogic" interactions within the matrix of relations with family, church, and community relations that bear on the mobilization of interdependent power. Or, put another way, repertoires are forged in a political process of action and reaction.

Most contests that draw on interdependent power unfold in this dancelike manner, as each side draws on accustomed strategies, and also responds and adapts its repertoire as it copes with the strategies of contenders. The fabled Pullman Strike of 1894 was precipitated by a string of wage cuts. When the company fired a committee of workers who petitioned for relief, the entire workforce walked out. Eugene Debs, leader of the American Railway Union (ARU), was cautious, but he sent the leader of the Railway Conductors to help the Pullman workers. The strikers managed to get a good deal of multilateral political support from the Civic Federation of Chicago, as well as help with provisions for the families of strikers. Even Chicago's mayor supported the workers, as did most Chicago labor union locals. Then the ARU convened and overrode Deb's caution by initiating a nationwide boycott of all trains carrying Pullman sleeping cars. But the railroad owners responded with a multilateral strategy of their own. Claiming that the railroads had been fought to a standstill, they raised the cry of interference with the U.S. mail, and called for federal intervention. The U.S. attorney general drew up an injunction against the ARU, and used a minor incident to call on the president to send federal troops who smashed the strike and destroyed the ARU.[30] For the time being, the railroad workers were defeated.

Charles Tilly has been preoccupied with the changing repertoires of popular action. His analysis implies that while repertoires are necessarily learned by participants and in this sense are culturally circumscribed, they are at least loosely determined by institutional arrangements. He was particularly concerned to account for the nineteenth-century transition from local and defensive forms of popular struggle to national proactive strategies such as the strike and the electoral rally. He saw the changing forms of popular action as a reflection of the emergence of the big structures of capitalism and of the nation-state, which shaped the "logic of the situation" that people confronted.[31]

Over the long term, the growth of capitalism and the national state did change the form of popular struggles (although it should also be pointed out that older forms of struggle persisted, particularly among marginal groups[32]). The food riot became unusual, the mass strike and the rally typical. Like Tilly, we usually attribute these changes to large-scale economic or political transformations, to the rise of industrial capitalism, or the nation-state, or to the complex of changes we call globalization. Restated in the terms of interdependent power, industrialism meant the erosion of a power nexus between large landowners and the rural poor, and the emergence of interdependencies between capital and industrial workers; the rise of the nation-state meant that a feudal ruling class lost power and a new power nexus emerged between state leaders and national publics. Globalization may make the interdependence between capital and labor in the First World less salient as capital spreads across the globe creating new interdependencies between capital and new groups of workers in the Southern Hemisphere.

However, a focus on big structures and big changes can also lead to a simplistic structural determinism. Economic and political change can alter power relations not only because big institutions are transformed, but because particular concrete interdependencies erode, and also because the very specific conditions that govern the actualization of interdependent power change. People recognize their leverage over particular employers or particular state leaders, not over capital in general or the state in general, although they are surely influenced by more general ideas about the relationship of employers to employees and of citizens to governments. They recognize commonalities and capacities for collective action among members of particular concrete groups far more readily than among the working class in general, although here, too, broader group identities and antagonisms may predispose them one way or the other. And people fear the loss of particular forms of employment to which they have access and in the particular places where their lives are rooted, although, once again, they are surely more likely to be alert to these dangers if they think capital exit is a more widespread phenomenon.

The shift from hand-loom to machine weaving in nineteenth-century England is an example, for it did not mean that manufacturers no longer depended on the English working class, but it did mean that the particular workers, the men who were the hand-loom weavers and the framework-knitters, could be abandoned as manufacturers turned to women and children to work in the new textile mills. And as this happened, the understandings, forms of solidarity, and strategies for limiting exit threats by employers that had developed in an earlier era of putting-out manufacturing also eroded.

Similarly, in our time, while capital still depends on labor in general, ongoing economic changes are undermining the specific ideas, solidarities, and strategies for curbing exit threats that were developed by concrete groups under the concrete circumstances of industrial capitalism. The old occupational categories—the miners, the steelworkers, the dockers, and so on—that were at the forefront of labor struggles have been depleted. And those who remain may no longer have the confidence that they can act to "shut it down," paralyze an industry, much less make an entire economy falter. Meanwhile, the working-class towns and neighborhoods are emptying out, and the particular working-class culture they nourished is fading. The unions that drew on all of this are necessarily enfeebled. They are enfeebled even more by employer strategies that take advantage of the decline of older forms of working-class power to launch new and terrifying exit threats—by hiring contingent workers and strike replacements, by restructuring production, or by threatening to close plants and shift production elsewhere.

But these discouraging developments may be less the result of the collapse of interdependent power in a postindustrial and transnational economy than of the maladaptation of the popular strategies or repertoires forged in an earlier industrial and nation-based economy. To be sure, miners, manufacturing workers, and dockers have lost numbers. However, these diminishing numbers are now lodged in systems of production that outsourcing and just-in-time inventories have made far more fragile. And the Internet and service workers who are becoming more numerous have only begun to explore the potential of their disruptive power in a densely interwoven national and international economy.

A consideration of the importance of repertoires in guiding popular collective action directs us to the possibility that there can be a large gap between institutionally created possibilities for power and the actual strategies that emerge. In the real world, the translation of institutional change into new popular political repertoires is fraught with difficulty. For one thing, as the term *repertoire* suggests, once-constructed strategies tend to persist because they become imprinted in cultural memory and habit, because they are reiterated by the organizations and leaders formed in past conflicts, and because strategies are shaped and constrained by the rules promulgated in response to earlier conflicts. People inevitably cling to accustomed modes of action, particularly when these have been at least partly successful in realizing their interests. This drag of the past is particularly true of subordinate groups, and it constrains the adjustment of strategy to changes in "big structures." Only slowly, through the experience of defeat and repression on the one hand, and the contingencies of imagination, invention, and the welling up of anger and defiance on the other, do new repertoires emerge that respond to new institutional conditions.

The Mob and the State

Disruptive Power and the Construction of American Electoral-Representative Arrangements

THE ELEMENTAL disruptive challenge takes the form of the mob, of the physical threat of the defiant crowd, and disorderly crowds figure largely in the history of disruptive movements, especially before the emergence of electoral-representative arrangements. The mob or the riot had, in fact, been a feature of communal politics for centuries, and it continues to this day to be a characteristic form of popular political action, particularly in the Southern Hemisphere and among the American poor. Perhaps at first glance, the riot seems not to fit my understanding of disruptive power as rooted in institutionalized relationships, but even the riot depends on the withdrawal of cooperation, in this case cooperation in the routines of communal or civic life.

The unruly mob played a large, albeit complicated, role in the American revolutionary war. Crowd actions were familiar in the eighteenth century, and "mobbing," as it was called, was the main repertoire that the American colonists brought with them from Europe, "a feature," says James Morone, of eighteenth-century communal life, both in the New World and the Old."[1]

In the years leading up to the Revolutionary War, American elites restless with British rule struck up an alliance with the mob, an alliance that came to be justified by radical democratic ideas about the people's rights to self-governance. Without the support of the mob, of the rabble, the war with England could not have been won.[2] It was they, after all, who provided the troops who fought the war. Moreover, the influence of the mob was imprinted on the provisions of the new state constitutions that reflected the reigning principles of radical democracy, and then, more dimly, on those provisions of the new federal constitution which spoke to popular rights and representation, provisions that had to be conceded to win support for the new national government.

The mobs of the revolutionary era struck out at local targets, against press gangs, landowners, local gentry, or cargo ships. But the outcome of their actions, of their attempts to exercise power, were importantly determined by the responses of more distant governments, including colonial governments, the British government, and ultimately the state-building elites who designed the American government. I will say more about the interplay of disruption and government response in the revolutionary era shortly, but before I do, I want to make some general observations about the large role that governments play in the dynamics of mobilizing disruptive power and in shaping the outcomes of disruptive challenges.

Government, because it is the seat of law, and of the legitimate use of force that makes the law so potent, is almost always involved in the politics of disruptive movements. Sometimes government is the direct target of the disruptors, but even if it is not, even when the targets are the landowners or the industrialists, the role of government looms large. For one thing, the framework of rules or constraints which delimits the exercise of popular power in the workplace or the community is ultimately lodged in government. Government has the legal authority and coercive force to define who can do what to whom, and thus to curb—but sometimes to permit—the exercise of power in interdependent relations.[3]

Government therefore plays a large role in managing—often suppressing, but sometimes legitimating—disruptive power challenges when these occur. But if the challenge surmounts these restraints, government can also become acutely vulnerable even when it is not the target of the challengers. The disruption of particular social relations reverberates widely in a densely interconnected society, creating conflict and polarization which may undermine political authority and fragment governing coalitions, threatening the power bases of particular state-based elites. Thus, economic disruptions such as strikes, or disruptions of civic order such as riots, can force new issues to the surface, and can activate and polarize groups that were heretofore cooperative or quiescent.

Government must respond to these disruptions in the first instance because state authority and power ultimately depend on the relatively smooth functioning of societal patterns of cooperation. If production shuts down, the contemporary "tax state" loses a portion of its revenues, and may well also lose the support of those whose profits or wages are in jeopardy.[4] In other words, government, especially modern government, is locked into complex societal systems of cooperation and interdependency.

But there are times when government lacks the authority and the military capacity to suppress or moderate disruptive challenges. As many have pointed out, the ability of a government to deal with domestic insurgency can be weakened because it is entangled in foreign war, or because its elite supporters are divided. The mob was as significant as it was in the American Revolution, because state power was weakened by the deepening conflict between colonial elites and the British crown, as well as with the British merchant interests who were influential with the crown. State power was also weakened by the vast distance that separated the colonies from the governing apparatus and military forces of the mother country, and by the fragmentation of colonial governing authorities.

Long before the emergence of electoral-representative arrangements, the periodic mobilization of interdependent power was the impetus for conciliation and concessions by ruling groups to those at the bottom-end of hierarchical relations. Indeed, the prevalence under feudal arrangements of the understanding that not only did people owe fealty and service to the lord, but that the lord also owed fealty and services to his subordinates, suggests at least a tacit acknowledgement of the workings of interdependent power. In turn, a culture that emphasized the reciprocal rights of feudal elites and the peasantry may well have made it easier to think about popular rights.[5] "Peasant revolts," writes Marc Bloch, "appear to be an inseparable part of the seigneurial regime, much as strikes are part of the modern capitalist enterprise."[6] People without wealth or control of force were granted some rights because their quiescence and cooperation could not always be taken for granted.

Over the course of the centuries-long change from feudal to commercial and then industrial capitalism, it was the rulers rather than the ruled who typically initiated violations of this compact of reciprocal obligation. The rural population responded with its own distinctive forms of defiance, tending to devise strategies that reflected the paths for influence made available by interdependent social relations. This was a tumultuous and disorderly politics, as people on both sides of lord and vassal relations, or employer and worker relations, or consumer and merchant relations, or citizen and magistrate relations, periodically withdrew their contributions to economic and political life, and even more generally as the numerous poor used the elemental interdependence yielded by physical proximity to force the concessions that might permit their survival.

Think for example of the episodes of popular defiance that marked the centuries-long transition from a feudal to a commercial economy in Europe, and that forced the creation of poor-relief systems.[7] Massive changes were taking place in the feudal order of western Europe as a rural population surplus combined with emerging market opportunities to prompt landowners to begin to renege on their feudal obligations and force the peasantry off the land. In this sense, the initiating rule-breakers were the landed elites who spurned medieval rules and custom, a point that is often reiterated in accounts of preindustrial crowd actions.

In response, the poor, who were prohibited by law from vagrancy and beggary, took to the road nevertheless. Starving rural people flocked to the towns, where they laid siege to the wealthy burghers with their pleas for alms and with their thievery, and where their very presence was threatening because disease epidemics often followed in the wake of hunger. Vagrancy, begging, and theft can be understood as something more than blind responses by the poor to their desperation.[8]

"The permanent confrontation with the migrating possessionless became an obsession for the 'right-minded' European," say Lis and Soly, and the more so when bad harvests or the expropriation of smallholders made the poor more numerous and more threatening.[9] Elemental and brutal as these interactions may have been, they were an effort by the poor, cast out of the feudal contract, to use their very physical being to force some accommodation by the better off to their desperate need. Their protests had consequences across Europe and particularly in England as local and national governmental authorities mobilized themselves to deal with the disturbances. Prohibitions and punishments for the poor were elaborated, and they were complemented by a developed institutional system for the provision of relief.[10] Karl Polanyi concluded of England that, "by and large the nearly 16,000 Poor Law authorities in the country managed to keep the social fabric of village life unbroken and undamaged."[11]

As the enclosure of common lands proceeded during the eighteenth century, the English rural poor continued to lose access to the land. Moreover, both in England and on the continent, local food supplies became more insecure after scarce harvests because the Crown's agents frequently commandeered them to feed the growing retinues of government employees and armies, or dealers commandeered them to sell the grain in the burgeoning cities. The main chroniclers of the food riots that ensued emphasize that the removal of local food supplies at times of shortage violated medieval custom and law. In this sense, it was again the elites who were taking the initiative and violating customary rules.

The indignant crowds that seized hordes of grain were, Rudé says, resisting "the new-fangled doctrine that the price of the necessities of life should be regulated by supply and demand rather than by a traditional concern for 'justice.'"[12] And the crowds often resisted by reenacting the traditional practices by which local magistrates had previously controlled prices during periods of dearth. Indeed, Tilly reports that the script was precise; the crowd assembled when the local market opened and merely seized the bread to which traditional practice entitled them, or sold it at a "just price."[13] Rudé and Tilly are writing about the general European experience. E. P. Thompson, discussing specifically English food riots, argues similarly that the script the crowd followed was not only customary but was actually embodied in an eroded body of statute law.[14]

Perhaps. But this emphasis on the influence of custom diverts attention from the fact that the food riot was also an effort to use interdependent power, to mobilize the contributions of common people to the cooperative activities of the local market, and to mobilize those contributions not only by following some of the rules but by breaking other rules, specifically the rules which gave authority to the magistrates. Nor were the resulting market disruptions without effect. To be sure, the poor did not reverse the spread of market relations or the growth of the cities or of the national state, the trends that provoked their resistance. But riots did force hoarded grain to be brought to market, and they intimidated farmers, brokers, and local officials who then moderated rising prices, at least for a time.[15] And the experience of the food riots probably contributed to the seriousness with which European governments attended to preventing local famines once the necessary transportation infrastructure became available.

My point, however, is not that disruptive power prevails. In fact, in the instances I have cited, it did not prevail. At most, it moderated the power of ruling groups. And it did not always succeed even in that. The Chartist movement was defeated. It did not succeed in reversing the draconian 1834 amendments to the Poor Law that had been perhaps the main goad to the protests. The Chartists were also motivated by ideas of democracy similar to those that undergirded popular agitation during the American Revolution. Their demands were fueled by an earlier movement for an expanded suffrage that preceded the Reform Act of 1832. The act was a bitter disappointment to the democratic hopes of British working people because, while it expanded suffrage, it also established the possession of property or a regular income as a condition of the right to vote. The Chartists mobilized around a platform of specifically political reform, demanding not only the universal male suffrage, but a remarkable agenda of parliamentary reforms.[16] "For ten years from 1838 to 1848 the authorities in Britain were faced with a popular movement which came nearer to being a mass rebellion than any other movement in modern times," writes Dorothy Thompson.[17] But universal male suffrage was won only slowly, and then long after the Chartist movement had faded. As for their radical democratic agenda for an accountable parliament, that was never achieved.

However, it is the American experience, and the role of disruptive power in the formation of the American state on which I wish to focus, and to which I now turn.

By the mid-eighteenth century, there were some 1.6 million Europeans in the colonies. Most of them came from England, and most were common folk, artisans, apprentices, sailors, laborers, urban poor, hard-scrabble farmers, and bonded servants and apprentices. They brought with them to the New World, as Tocqueville pointed out, the relatively egalitarian ideas that had nourished Protestant dissent in England for a century.[18] They also carried with them the popular political repertoire of eighteenth-century England, with its reliance on mob action. "Its most dramatic recurrent forms," writes Charles Tilly of eighteenth-century collective actions, "were the food riot, concerted resistance to conscription, organized invasions of fields and forests, and rebellion against tax-collectors." Its "exotic features" included "displays of effigies and symbols of the crowd's enemies, or the ritual sacking of a wrongdoer's dwelling" and the "recurrent adoption of the authorities own expected means of action (in mock trials and executions, for instance, or in the seizure of grain for public sale which lay at the center of many food riots)."[19]

Benjamin Franklin, observing the crowd actions in London that accompanied the electoral success of the remarkable and defiant John Wilkes in 1768, wrote of the "Madness of English Mobs." But American mobs were at least as mad, perhaps madder, and conditions allowed them to be so. England, after all, had a well-developed state apparatus, a self-confident and united ruling class, a legal system and national system of royal courts, and an army. The colonies, however, were separated from this apparatus by 3,000 miles and a long ocean journey. The colonial governments, by contrast with England, were often fractious, were riddled by divisions between royal governors and elected assemblies, and were also relatively open and democratic. Perhaps upward of 50 percent of white males were enfranchised (in contrast to England where only 15 percent of adult men elected representatives to the House of Commons[20]), many of the colonies had annual elections and, according to Morone, they even allowed voters to give specific instructions on issues to the assembly.[21]

The great distance from Britain, and the relatively loose and open governmental authority in the colonies, probably made it easier for common people to recognize their contributions to interdependent social relations, and easier also to defy the rules which governed their participation.[22] They brought the repertoire of mobbing with them from eighteenth-century England, but they certainly drew on it frequently once they were here:

> Eighteenth-century Americans accepted the existence of popular uprisings with remarkable ease. Riots and tumults, it was said, happened "in all governments at all times." . . . Not that extra-legal uprisings were encouraged. They were not. But in certain circumstances, it was understood, the people would rise up almost as a natural force, much as night follows day, and this phenomenon often contributed to the public welfare.[23]

"[C]olonial mobs," says Edward Countryman of the prerevolutionary period, "were a fact of life,"[24] and popular action in the form of riots and tumults long preceded the Revolutionary War. Bacon's Rebellion of white frontiersmen joined by slaves and servants on the Virginia frontier occurred only seventy years after the colony was founded, in 1676. The British crown responded by sending 1,000 soldiers across the Atlantic, the rebellion was suppressed, and the leaders were hanged. But, according to Howard Zinn, in the next hundred years there were eighteen other uprisings aimed at overthrowing colonial governments, six black rebellions, and forty riots.[25]

Ray Raphael writes of the crowds protesting British impressments, gangs who swept the waterfronts of the coastal towns from time to time in the 1740s. In 1741, a Boston crowd angered by impressments responded by beating up a sheriff and stoning a justice of the peace. In 1742, protesters attacked the commander of the *Astrea* and destroyed a Royal Navy barge. In 1745, they pummeled the commander of the

HMS *Shirley* and left a deputy sheriff unconscious. In 1747, when fifty British sailors deserted from the HMS *Lark*, the crowd responded to efforts to find them by putting a deputy sheriff in the stocks and seizing the officers of the *Lark* as hostages, so frightening the governor that he fled his mansion for an island in the harbor. The crowd remained in control of the city until the governor negotiated the release of most of the impressed seamen. "Common people," writes Raphael, "felt well within their rights to liberate impressed seamen or commandeer a few loaves of overpriced bread."[26]

As the eighteenth century wore on, tensions were increasing in the colonies, not only in relations with the British, but among the colonists themselves.[27] As the population grew, sectional differences of interest emerged, and inequalities grew sharper, both in rural areas as large landowners confronted tenant farmers and the landless poor, and in the cities where wealth was becoming more concentrated and, as it did, riotous crowd actions increased.[28] One study found evidence of 150 riots in the 13 colonies in the period from 1765 to 1769, defining a riot as a gathering of 12 or more people "to assert their will immediately through the use of force outside the normal bounds of law."[29] Mobs and their "violence," writes Schlesinger, "played a dominant role at every significant turning point of the events leading up to the War for Independence."[30] "What is striking about the outbursts," adds Morone, "is their political ambiguity: they challenged both English policy and colonial elites."[31]

Events in the decade and a half before the Revolution helped to paper over these differences, leading to at least a temporary alliance between colonial elites antagonized by British policies and the mob.[32] British officials in the colonies were quick to see this. "It is incredible," wrote Thomas Gage in 1765, "the great pains that have been taken to raise people of all ranks against the stamp."[33] The governor of Massachusetts made the larger point in 1766 that leaders "have labored so successfully, that the very principles of the common people are changed, and they now form to themselves pretension and expectations which had never entered their heads a year or two ago."[34]

Popular discontent was growing, but so was anger among colonial merchants and landowners, precipitated in large part by the British

Crown's efforts to rationalize its colonial policies. In 1763, the Crown decided to maintain a standing army in the colonies. Shortly afterward, in an effort to crack down on pervasive smuggling and the lax payment of taxes, new taxes were introduced, colonial assemblies were required to billet British troops, and an effort was made to curb the authority of colonial assemblies. At first, protests from the colonies against the Stamp Act of 1765 led the Parliament to back down. The Parliament also withdrew the Townshend duties of 1767 in the wake of an extended boycott of British goods by American merchants. But the British government persisted in its campaign with the Sugar Act, the Tea Act, and another Stamp Act, and also by introducing new tax agents and increasingly tough administrative requirements. In response, colonial resistance escalated, each side reacting to the other, as well as to the multiple domestic interests that had to be accommodated on each side of the Atlantic.

The mob played a crucial role in this rising resistance movement. "Crowds made it impossible to enforce the Stamp Act; they gave power to the nonimportation agreements that merchants adopted against the Townshend taxes; they dumped East India tea into more than one harbor."[35] Then, in 1773, when a Boston mob dumped the East India Company's tea to prevent the payment of duties, the British didn't back down and demanded that the Bostonians pay for the tea. Edward Countryman says that this is when the "final rupture began."[36]

The approach of war with England only fueled popular democratic aspirations. Wars are declared by elites, but they are fought by ordinary people. Sometimes the foot soldiers figure out that war-making, by making leaders more acutely dependent on them, has given them greater power.[37] This awareness must have been heightened during the revolutionary period because the people who took up arms, or those who otherwise suffered the real hardships of war, were gripped by the new passion for democracy. Demands spread even for the democratic election of militia officers, and in 1775 the Continental Congress acknowledged the urgency of the demand by recommending that officers below the rank of field officers be elected by their men.[38] In the election of 1775, unqualified tenants as well as underage males turned up at the White Plains, New York, courthouse to vote.[39] And in 1780, the officers of the Sixth Company of Militia in the Third Regiment of Suffolk County wrote the Massachusetts governor in fury that a new constitution established a sixty-pound property qualification for the vote. Their fellow soldiers, they wrote, "who are so poor as to be thus deprived of their fundamental Rights, [although] . . . they are fighting for their own freedom."[40] For Americans of the time, says Gordon Woods, "politics was nothing more than a perpetual battle between the passions of the rulers, whether one or a few, and the united interest of the people."[41]

The democratic idea, to be sure, had fired the popular imagination before.[42] It spurred the Levelers and Diggers in Cromwell's New Model Army to rise up against the Crown in the seventeenth century.[43] It moved the workers and peasants of France at the end of the eighteenth century to call for a "Democratic and Social Republic." And it inspired mechanics, farmers, and laborers to take up arms in the American revolution. It also inspired them—and this in the context of a polity still organized on the principles of class deference—to demand some democratic rights. The motivating idea was simple and compelling. If ordinary people could participate in selecting state leaders, they would be able to control the exercise of the formidable power of their governments, including the power to tax, to imprison debtors, and to raise armies. "Whatever is good for the People," Thomas Gordon, an English radical, had written, "is bad for their Governors; and what is good for the Governors, is pernicious to the People."[44] "Democracy's promise is so attractive," comment Guidry and Sawyer, "that persons or groups who suffer political exclusion under democratic and nondemocratic regimes alike still appeal to the same notions of equality, citizenship, liberty and self-governance in order to make claims in public policies."[45]

The new state constitutions written after the revolutionary war broke out reflected the egalitarian and libertarian ideas that were spreading up and down the eastern seaboard. The radical democrats of the period sought to guarantee popular liberty by creating constitutions that limited executive power, provided unicameral legislatures or at least powerful lower houses that did not privilege the propertied, specified short terms of office that would force elected officials to confront the people who elected them frequently, and required open legislative deliberations by a local and accessible government. These sorts of arrangements were understood as ways of ensuring that officials remained accountable to the mass electorates that put them in office.

Keyssar's account of constitution-making in Pennsylvania makes clear that the outbreak of war, by revealing the dependence of elites on ordinary men, fueled democratic aspirations:

> The key actors in the drama were members of the highly politicized Philadelphia militias who seized the early initiative in Pennsylvania's rejection of British rule. As early as March 1776, the Committee of Privates, speaking of rank-and-file militiamen drawn from the city's "lower" and "middling sorts," announced its readiness to discard colonial suffrage requirements. . . . Later in the spring, the committee also demanded that militiamen be permitted to elect their own officers, and that all taxpaying militia associators be allowed to vote for delegates who would draw up the new constitution.[46]

As a result, Pennsylvania actually adopted a unicameral legislature whose members were elected annually, and it abandoned property ownership as the basis for the franchise.[47]

Eight states adopted new constitutions during 1776, and three other states acted the following year. All of the new constitutions limited the prerogatives of executives and the courts and enlarged the powers of the legislatures, which became the main governmental authorities. These legislatures, says Gordon Wood, "were probably as equally and fairly representative of the people as any legislature in history."[48] Democratic legislatures, in turn, generated in the 1780s a rash of legislation for relieving debtors, confiscating property, and printing money.[49]

American elites were increasingly alarmed. As early as 1776, John Adams had warned

> Depend on it, Sir, it is dangerous to open so fruitful a source of controversy and altercation as would be opened by attempting to alter the qualifications of voters; there will be no end of it. New

claims will arise . . . and every man who has not a farthing, will demand an equal voice with any other, in all acts of state. It tends to confound and destroy all distinctions, and prostrate all ranks to one common level.[50]

Alarm in turn precipitated a wave of efforts to reform the new state constitutions. In New York, New Hampshire, and Massachusetts, for example, provisions for a strong Senate and an independent executive were introduced to tame the lower house. Similar efforts were made, with mixed success, in other states in a campaign to rein in what were considered the democratic excesses of the earlier constitutions.[51]

Once the war with England had been won, the latent divisions between colonial elites and the lesser sorts of artisans, laborers, and farmers emerged more clearly. The outbreak of rebellion in western Massachusetts in 1786 brought these brewing conflicts to a head, at least in the minds of American elites. Farmers already burdened by postwar depression and debt faced a steep increase in poll and property taxes imposed by the state legislature. The farmers gathered to draft resolutions pleading for relief. When the legislature did not respond, armed mobs closed the courts to halt debtor suits in the effort to keep their farms. The rebellion spread to other parts of New England. The next year, rebel forces under Daniel Shays attempted to seize the Continental arsenal at Springfield. The rebels were dispersed, but the annual election required by the Massachusetts constitution intervened, voter turnout nearly tripled, and rebel sympathizers gained majorities in the legislature. The rebels were given amnesty, taxes were lowered, and most debtors were released from prison.[52]

Here was dramatic evidence in the view of elites that larger solutions were needed to tame the excesses of democracy unleashed by the Revolution. Even before the rebellion, elite reformers had come to the conclusion that "reform of the national government was the best means of remedying the evils caused by the state governments. . . . The calling of the Philadelphia convention was the climax of the process . . . that had begun with the reformation of the state constitutions."[53] The Shays episode only strengthened the resolve of the nation-building elite reformers.

To be sure, there were other problems that preoccupied the founders in their endeavors. The Articles of Confederation were proving to be an unwieldy apparatus for enforcing repayment of the debts to wealthy supporters incurred by the revolutionary army, or even more important in the longer run, the articles did not provide the authority needed to construct the governmental structures that would support their rising commercial and national ambitions.[54] The most important change, therefore, entailed by the writing and adoption of the Constitution was the very creation of a national government with the necessary powers. The men who gathered behind closed doors in Philadelphia designed a new government with the authority to protect and enhance private property by regulating and protecting trade and the currency; by repaying the loans that had funded the revolutionary army; by improving roads, canals, and harbors; and by organizing the military forces that would protect American seafaring commerce and secure the western lands against Native Americans.

This was not all, however. The excesses of the state governments that had fallen under the sway of radical democracy also instructed the framers in their nation-building ambitions. The radical democrats had fought for small electoral districts and a government accessible to ordinary people. By the same reasoning, the constitution-makers worked to create a distant government that would preside over the people as a whole, a huge constituency, fully aware that these arrangements would favor the participation of the affluent and connected and remove government from the disorderly rabble. "Only an examination of the Federalists' social perspective, their fears and anxieties about the disarray in American society, can fully explain how they conceived of the Constitution as a political device designed to control the social forces the Revolution had released."[55]

The constitutional arrangements that were designed to solve these different problems were proposed at a moment when democratic passions still ran high, among an armed people. The challenge was to conciliate popular feeling, while also limiting influence by the ordinary people who had taken up arms against the British. The resulting arrangements were intricate. There had to be democratic concessions, but they also had to be limited if the property-oriented problems that motivated nation building were to be solved. Given the democratic temper of the times, and the absence of either the armed forces or the legal majesty of a developed state, this was a delicate matter indeed.

To cope with the difficulties posed when policies dealing with the crucial matters of foreign and interstate trade, currency, and the repayment of loans were in the hands of runaway state legislatures, authority over the policies dealing with these and other matters affecting business and trade was explicitly assigned to the new federal government in Article I, Section 8 of the Constitution, a set of measures that Parenti points out was passed easily and without argument by the assembled framers.[56]

All residual policy authority remained with the states, an arrangement that at the time was a concession to established political practice, and to Anti-Federalist sentiment. This was to turn out to be extraordinarily important because it established the United States as a *federal* system.[57] The states, and municipal governments as well, retained taxing and spending authority in many areas of governance. This meant that even while crucial economic policies were centralized, other policies remained decentralized. State and local politics remained vigorous in the United States, and that vigor resulted from the fact that these subnational governments did indeed do many things. However, the strength of subnational governments had ironic consequences, although the framers could scarcely have anticipated this. Over time, as the economy grew, subnational governments became easy prey to the pressures of corporate interests that backed their policy demands by the threat to move the jobs and tax revenues they controlled beyond state or city borders.[58]

Following the model of the reformed state constitutions, a Senate was created whose members would have long terms, in contrast to the precepts of radical democracy which emphasized that the people should be able to recall their representatives swiftly. And the presidency was established as the chief executive of the new government.

Since the new government had to be justified in democratic terms as representative of the people, both the executive and the legislature would be elected. But the electoral arrangements for the president and the Senate gave the people only an indirect role. The Senate was in effect an upper chamber, with senators chosen by state legislatures.[59] The president was chosen by the electoral college. Thus both Senate and president were selected by a process that filtered popular influence through the more prominent men who were more likely to gain office as legislators or electors. The influence of popular majorities was further blunted by staggering elections for these different positions. Finally, representation was sharply skewed away from the population in favor of the states who were guaranteed equal representation in the Senate. The electoral college was also weighted to favor states, and it would be almost two centuries before the "one man, one vote" rule was applied to House districts.[60]

The People's House was the House of Representatives, whose members were to be chosen by direct election every two years, a provision that more nearly reflected the precepts of radical democracy. States retained control of the franchise here as elsewhere, but the Constitution specified that those with the right to vote for the most numerous branch of the state legislature were entitled to vote for members of the House.[61] This was the main concession to democratic feeling. Even here, however, radical democratic principles were sharply compromised. House constituencies were huge, where the radical democrats had insisted on small districts, and these large constituencies favored aspirants of stature, wealth, and visibility.[62]

Then there was the judiciary, which in short order claimed ultimate authority in interpreting the Constitution and thus became a coequal branch.[63] Not only did the Supreme Court assume the authority to veto actions by the other branches and the states, but "in the guise of reviewing the constitutionality of state and congressional actions or inactions, the federal judiciary would later engage in what in some instances could also only be called judicial policy making—or, if you like, judicial legislation."[64] The judges who assumed this authority were simply appointed, and they enjoyed life tenure. Over time, the decisions of the Court were to become crucial in protecting the propertied from governmental interference in response to popular pressures.

These limits on popular majorities were complemented by the famous division of powers among the branches of this new government. Wood characterizes this as a design "to prevent the emergence of any "common passion" or sense of oneness among large numbers of persons. . . ."[65] As Alexander Hamilton explained in Federalist Paper No. 60, "The House of Representatives . . . elected immediately by the people, the Senate by the State legislatures, the President by electors chosen for that purpose by the people, there would be little probability of a common interest to cement these different branches in a predilection for any particular class of electors."

The founders began the Constitution with the resounding words "We the people . . ." The success of the campaign they waged to secure ratification at state conventions hung on their democratic rhetoric, on the argument that not only the legislature, but all parts of this new government, would somehow represent the people. They adopted "the radical theory of the sovereignty of the people; in the name of the people they engineered a conservative counter-revolution and erected a nationalistic government whose purpose in part was to thwart the will of 'the people' in whose name they acted."[66] And although forced to concede the Bill of Rights, which had not been intended, they mounted a heavy-handed campaign that Jackson Turner Main thinks secured the adoption of the constitution despite the probable opposition of a majority of the population.[67]

Volumes have been written about the American Constitution and the multiple ways that its provisions blocked or channeled popular influence. Although Americans may think it was the model for other nations, many of the arrangements I have highlighted remained unique among democratic nations.[68] But my main point for now is not that popular power was limited by constitution-making, which it surely was. Rather, my point is that the disruptive power challenges of the revolutionary period could not be ignored either. At the outset of their deliberations, the gentlemen assembled in Philadelphia had considered proposals by Hamilton to give lifetime tenure to senators and the president, the better to distance the new government from democratic currents. Under the circumstances, they did not dare. Instead, they conceded a republican form of government with neither property nor religious qualifications for its officials, whose terms were also explicitly limited. And in the exigencies of battling for their proposals, they also conceded key popular liberties, including freedom of speech and religion; the right to assemble peaceably and to petition for redress of grievances, freedom from unreasonable searches and seizures, and a series of protections in legal proceedings. "[T]he notion," writes Keyssar, "that a legitimate government required the 'consent' of the governed became a staple of political thought; and a new, contagious language of rights and equality was widely heard."[69]

Moreover, in the decades following the adoption of the Constitution, the suffrage expanded. The framers had forced the issue of establishing the prerequisites for suffrage onto the states, and in the states, property requirements largely collapsed, albeit not all at once. Property requirements were at first replaced with taxpaying requirements, but these too were gradually eliminated. By the 1830s, most white men had at least gained the right to vote.[70]

"At bottom," writes Barrington Moore, the Revolution "was a fight between commercial interests in England and America," and its "main effect was to promote unification of the colonies" and their separation from England.[71] But this was not the whole of it. True, the American national government was the construction of elites, craftily arranged to hold the colonies together. But it occurred in the aftermath of a war that had required the mass mobilization of ordinary people and the encouragement of democratic ideas. "It seems unlikely," writes Edmund Morgan, "that the political, social, and cultural changes wrought in the name of equality since 1776 could have occurred under British rule. It was the Founders who made them possible by defying a king and creating a republic."[72] The constitution registered these influences as well. What was remarkable about these events was not only the intelligence and ambition of the elites, but that the mob had played a large if convoluted role in the construction of a new state with at least some of the elemental features of democracy.[73]

Once constructed, these new institutional arrangements did not simply suppress future disruptive challenges. Rather, the politics of electoral-representative institutions sometimes encouraged future outbreaks of disruptive protest. And electoral politics became the arena in which the impact of disruption was registered and measured, and responses to it molded. I will examine these dynamics as they unfolded in the extraordinary nineteenth-century campaign for emancipation.

CHAPTER

FOUR

✦
❦

Dissensus Politics, or the Interaction of Disruptive Challenges with Electoral Politics
The Case of the Abolitionist Movement

ONCE ELECTORAL-REPRESENTATIVE arrangements exist, popular disruptive challenges of any consequence inevitably become entangled with electoral politics. "Party structure" say Garner and Zald, "is probably the single most important variable for understanding the pattern of social movements. . . . Both are organizational forms for pursuing political ends, so it is not surprising that they are so closely intertwined."[1] They are indeed intertwined, but the dynamic of their interaction is not obvious.

On the one side, politicians running for office are sometimes led to give voice to the hopes and grievances of particular discontented groups. Electoral politics therefore constitutes a large part of the discursive political environment that gives rise to and shapes disruptive movements. On the other side, the movements can have a large effect on the fortunes of electoral contenders. This is partly because collective defiance leads to institutional disruptions that discomfit particular voter blocs or economic interests, as when the railroads stop running or access to public places is blocked. It is also because the drama of collective action, including the drama often created by the stoppages themselves, is likely to heighten attention to issues that were previously suppressed. The disruptive challenge enlists opinion on one side or the other of the newly inflamed issue. When the ensuing group polarization cuts across the lines of party affiliation, political leaders in an electoral-representative system are threatened with the potential fragmentation of their electoral support.

Protest movements thus activate opposition as well as support. This consequence is usually thought of as a main drawback of protest strategies. But it is not so simple as that. The disruption caused by movements may drive the groups that oppose them out of party coalitions and in this way reduce opposition to the protesters demands. The abolitionists shattered the intersectional Whig coalition by the furious opposition it aroused in the South. The new Republican Party that emerged did not include the powerful southern opponents of emancipation. The strike movement that arose in the 1930s with the rhetorical encouragement of the New Deal infuriated industrial leaders and destroyed the possibility of a business-Democratic alliance, opening the way for Democratic Party support of prolabor legislation. Similarly, the rise of civil rights protests in the South in the 1950s and 1960s not only elicited sympathy and support from northern Democrats but simultaneously aroused intransigent opposition, driving the white south out of the Democratic Party. Not only did this make civil rights concessions easier, but it heightened the importance of black voter support to party leaders.

The abolitionists played a major role in the convulsive events that led to the legal emancipation of African Americans, which Barrington Moore called "a partial victory for human freedom."[2] Even partial victory required a transformation of American politics. And although we often think of the abolitionists as idealists and ideologues, as wordsmiths and orators, they were also disruptive. Abolitionist agitation led to street fights and civil disorder, it created schisms in the major Protestant churches in which the movement activists were enmeshed, and abolitionists staffed the Underground Railway that infuriated the South because it threatened to bleed slaves from the southern system. At a time when sectional tensions were already rising, these disruptive challenges set in motion the tangled process of electoral dissensus that ultimately split apart the national intersectional parties, leading to a bloody civil war and the elimination of chattel slavery. In this chapter, I will draw on the experience of the abolitionists to illustrate the interplay of disruptive movements with electoral politics.

The Rise of Mass Parties

E. E. Schattschneider thought that constitutional arrangements worked against party building. The framers were famously leery of mass parties and the prospect of majority rule that they represented, and the elaborate division of powers in the national government, along with the resulting fragmentation of popular constituencies, was designed to thwart such parties. Thus authority in the national government was divided between the two houses of Congress, the presidency, and the courts, each of which was assigned distinct decision-making authority, and each of which was assigned different routes and different constituencies for accession to power. This system, said Schattschneider, was "designed to make parties ineffective . . . [because they] would lose and exhaust themselves in futile attempts to fight their way through the labyrinthine framework."[3] Schattschneider was right. Divided powers and divided routes to power, together with the substantial decentralization of authority to the states, had the effect of making parties weak and porous instruments of popular governance, easily penetrated by organized special interests.

But the Constitution that prevented responsible parties in policy terms nevertheless ensured that mass parties would develop because it laid the basis for a mass electorate. The Constitution provided that members of the House of Representatives would be elected by those eligible to vote for representatives to the lower houses of the state legislatures. With that stroke, the framers devolved conflicts over the right to vote, which the democratic fervor of the era ensured, to the states.

"Societies probably come closest to democracy," writes Colin Crouch, "in the early years after achieving it . . . when enthusiasm for it is widespread . . . when the powerful interests which dominate unde-mocratic societies are wrong-footed and thrown on the defensive."[4] Chilton Williamson says something similar. The revolutionary period "was the turning point in the conscious democratization of ideas about the suffrage and in the actual liberalization of colonial suffrage laws."[5] And in the decades that followed, restrictions on the white male suf-frage were toppled, one after the other. Property qualifications were replaced by taxpayer requirements, and then these too were relaxed.[6] Party competition between the Federalists, who represented merchants and bankers, and the Jeffersonian Republicans, who represented planters, contributed to this process, as the Republicans worked to gain support from hitherto excluded groups.[7] By the 1830s, the states had removed most restrictions on white male suffrage, and more state and local officials were exposed to periodic elections by the enfranchised population.[8] Popular suffrage in presidential elections was also liberal-ized. From 1812 to 1820, state legislatures selected electors in nine states. But as the number of states expanded, more states chose elec-tors through popular voting. By 1824, a majority of states chose presi-dential electors by popular vote.[9]

The mass franchise inevitably gives rise to mass political parties, and mass parties have become, in Sartori's words, "*the* central interme-diate and intermediary structure between society and government."[10] To be sure, there had been parties, in the sense of organized efforts by political leaders to exercise power, before the expansion of the fran-chise. John Aldrich says that by the Second Congress (1791–1793), most officeholders could be identified either as Federalists or as (Jeffersonian) Republicans, and by the Third Congress, voting patterns had polarized along these party lines.[11] These parties operated as caucuses of officials without a reliable mass base.

The expanding electorate prodded politicians seeking office to orga-nize a different kind of party, one designed not so much to govern as to mobilize and manipulate the voting majorities who would deliver control of government to party leaders and their allies. By 1828, the familiar techniques of the mass party—running popular heroes for office whose policy platforms were ambiguous or unknown, coupled with organized fund-raising; systematic patronage; reliance on mass media; and popular parades, speechmaking, and entertainments—were all in use. The techniques were pioneered by the Jacksonian Democrats under the leadership of Martin Van Buren of the Albany Regency. The Jacksonians drew together state-level party organizations to mobilize voters for both state and national power. The Whigs quickly followed suit, essentially copying the strategies of the Jacksonians.[12]

Behind the scenes, parties compiled master mailing lists of voters; mobilized state and local campaign committees; mustered the patronage brigades; and ground out posters, leaflets, and propaganda tracts. Fifteen hundred newspapers—most of them partisan weeklies—carried news of the party battle even to the frontier.[13]

The mass party, in turn, with its new techniques for mobilizing voters, increased voter turnout dramatically,[14] although the results certainly were not radical democracy. Charles Dickens, visiting the United States in 1842, characterized the political strategies of members of the Congress:

> Despicable trickery at elections; under-handed tamperings with public officers, cowardly attacks upon opponents with scurrilous newspapers for shields, and hired pens for daggers; shameful trucklings to mercenary knaves . . . in a word, Dishonest Faction in its most depraved and unblushing form.[15]

All of this, and especially the parades, the speeches, and the payoffs, has become the stuff of American political folklore. By the late 1830s, the basic features of the American electoral system had been constructed.

Electoral-representative institutions require political elites to mobilize large blocs of voters to retain or gain state authority, making them vulnerable to the fragmenting threats of disruptive movements. Polarization is particularly dangerous for leaders in a two-party system where success in any particular election depends on winning the support of a majority of voters. I have already noted the features of American electoral arrangements that sustain two-party politics, including single-member districts, plurality contests, the winner-take-all elections that result,[16] and the pervasive rigging of a range of election rules by the major parties to disadvantage third-party challengers. My objective here, however, is not to explain the institutional arrangements that drive third parties to the margin, but to point out that the majoritarian politics of a two-party system demands of politicians that they paste together unlikely coalitions, often in the face of a fractious and divided population, and these coalitions may be acutely susceptible to the divisions that result from the articulation of issues accompanying disruptive challenges.

Thus, while political elites must mobilize majorities, disruptive challengers work to fragment them. I call this process *dissensus*, and I think it is the key to understanding the power sometimes wielded by disruptive protests over public policy decisions in the United States. Notice, dissensus works not only, and sometimes not even mainly, because it mobilizes allies. Allies are important, to be sure; without them, disruptors can simply be crushed and their fracturing threat eliminated. But so is the activation of opposition important, and sometimes critical.

By arousing antagonists and spurring their defection from a majority coalition, the disruptors may change the calculus of electoral success, opening the way for policy concessions on the movement's issues. They may drive away their most strident opponents so that concessions become easier as worker disruptions succeeded in doing during the New Deal and as Civil Rights succeeded in doing in the 1960s. The defections spurred by disruption may also create a hole in the party's expected majority that prompts political leaders to turn to the disruptors and their allies to fill, as national Democrats turned to southern blacks in the effort to reconstruct their party's base in the 1960s. Notice, dissensus does not require that the movement organize majorities. It is a strategy for achieving political goals that can be mounted by the minorities slighted by majoritarian two-party politics.

The Electoral Context of Abolitionism

Although free blacks participated in the urban mobs of the revolutionary period, their numbers were few. Most of the African Americans in the United States were of course rural and enslaved, and not easily available for mobbing. Deborah Gray White estimates that the free black population numbered only 59,000 in 1790, although it grew to 488,000 by the beginning of the Civil War.[17] Once war with England broke out, both sides made efforts to recruit slaves with the promise of freedom, although the British tried harder. They were also more likely to honor their promises and were more successful, recruiting about twenty thousand African Americans. Far fewer served with the revolutionary army.[18] Some slaves took advantage of the war not to serve in the armies, but to escape. Thomas Jefferson estimated that twenty-five thousand Virginia slaves left their owners during the war.[19] Some formed maroon communities, although they were likely to be hunted down when the fighting stopped.[20]

These qualifications notwithstanding, the conflicts of the revolutionary period were overwhelmingly conflicts among whites. The ensuing constitutional pact that was the foundation of the American national state was multisided, to be sure, but it was a pact between whites. One compromise was struck between white elites and the white farmers, laborers, and mechanics who furnished recruits for the mob, and another between elites from northern and southern states. I have already discussed the outlines of the first compromise. The abolitionist movement was directed against the second, but the strategies through which it succeeded relied importantly on the electoral representative arrangements that had sealed the first compromise.

The draft of the Declaration of Independence that Thomas Jefferson presented to the Continental Congress in July 1776 included in its list of grievances against the British the Crown's support for the slave traffic. The southern delegates did not agree, and the clause was dropped.[21] After the war, when delegates from five southern states and eight northern states gathered in Philadelphia to write the Constitution, success again depended on reassuring the South that the new union would not jeopardize the slave system. James Madison himself acknowledged that the real differences of interest lay between the North and the South.[22]

The great danger to our general government is *the great southern and northern interests of the continent, being opposed to each other. Look to the votes in congress, and most of them stand divided by the geography of the country.*[23]

The egalitarian rhetoric of the revolutionary period could not have been reassuring to the southerners. "The problem of the South until its victory at the 1787 Convention," writes Staughton Lynd, was that, "recognizing the need for stronger Federal powers, it feared to create them until it was assured that the South could control their use."[24]

Key provisions in the new constitution were written to provide that assurance. The notorious three-fifths rule, by counting a slave as three-fifths of a person for purposes of allocating representation, gave the southern states "a large and domineering representation in Congress."[25] Southerners, says Gary Wills, made this "a nonnegotiable condition for their joining the Union."[26] Not only did this provision give the South increased representation in the House, but as Michael Goldfield points out, the three-fifths rule also gave owners of large numbers of slaves in black-majority counties the ability to control their state legislatures, and it was state legislatures that selected senators.[27] Moreover, disproportionate southern representation in Congress was reflected in the electoral college, with the consequence that most American presidents until the Civil War were southerners and slaveholders.[28]

There were other compromises in the sectional accord which made nation building possible, including a provision that allowed the importation of slaves to continue until 1808;[29] another that prohibited state laws from "impairing the obligations of contract," which was understood to protect property in slaves;[30] and another that required fugitive slaves to be returned to their owners. These provisions protecting slavery were not concessions to the South only. Although it was already clear that slavery was the peculiar institution of the South,[31] only the New England states and Pennsylvania had passed laws to end human bondage. Most states were slave states at the time of the constitutional convention, and slave holdings were understood to be protected by the Constitution. No small wonder that when the abolitionist movement arose, the more radical abolitionist leaders would conclude that emancipation would require the overturning of the Constitution itself.

The mass parties that emerged during the Jacksonian era were intersectional coalitions of state parties that included planter, commercial, banking, and manufacturing interests. There were important sectional differences among these economic interests regarding national policies on the tariff, internal improvements and westward expansion, banking, and later railroad policy. But there were powerful interests that spanned the division between North and South. The South was rich and growing richer. Slavery and cotton were enormously profitable. After the invention of the cotton gin in 1793, cotton production boomed, from nine thousand bales in 1791, to over a million by 1833, and to nearly five million bales by 1860.[32] Planter wealth in land and slaves increased commensurately.

Cotton wealth was not only important to the South. For the first third of the nineteenth century, the cotton trade was the most important spur to the growth of manufacturing. Barrington Moore writes of the nineteenth-century American economy that "slavery was no anachronistic excrescence on industrial capitalism. It was an integral part of this system and one of its prime motors in the world at large."[33] Growing northern electoral influence meant the possibility of northern influence over national policies, and, given sectional differences on a range of issues, this was a threat not only to the South, but to powerful northern interests with stakes in the wealth of the South.

Reflecting this reality, both the rules and the strategies of the parties reiterated the constitutional accommodation to the South and to slavery. Martin Van Buren, the Jacksonian strategist of party building, was keenly aware of the dangers of sectional conflict, perhaps unsurprisingly given the importance of the cotton trade to the New York banks.[34] Noting that party distinctions were inevitable, he underlined the importance of a national party that would link "planters of the South with plain Republicans of the North," reviving the Jeffersonian coalition, for otherwise party building risked "geographical divisions founded on local interests, or what is worse prejudices between free and slave holding states"[35] High-flown phrases aside, Van Buren argued in private correspondence that national parties were the means of keeping the slavery issue quiet.[36] At the core of his party-building strategy was an alliance between the Democratic organization that Van

Buren had built in New York and the Democratic organization in Virginia.[37]

Again, the Whigs followed suit. They not only adopted the mass organizing strategies of the Democrats, but they also adopted the strategies that suppressed sectional divisions. Vacuous or nonexistent party platforms were mirrored by the empty rhetoric of presidential candidates, allowing state and local leaders to attribute to the national party and its candidates whatever policies seemed advantageous with their electorates. This, combined with the considerable autonomy of state and local parties, made the intersectional party coalitions that dominated the "second-party system" possible. For both parties, issues that divided the sections sharply were dangerous, threatening party unity and election victories.

Such differences as were evident between the parties were not so much sectional as broadly economic. The Whigs tended to be more rooted in the commercial economy and more prosperous. As Marc Egnal writes, "Paradoxically, the issues separating the two parties helped promote intersectional cooperation. Party members in the North worked together with their Southern counterparts to forward or oppose an economic agenda. Sectional interests were present. But during the heyday of the second-party system they never threatened the very fiber of the Union because factions were not structured around regional concerns."[38]

Southern delegates to the constitutional convention had expected their minority status to be short-lived. The southern system would expand into the territories, and the territories in turn would be carved up into new states that would yield the southern section more representatives and more electoral votes.[39] In fact, the population of the North, swelled by immigration, grew faster. But the three-fifths rule nevertheless continued to sustain southern electoral votes at about 30 percent, giving the section effective influence in the Congress and the presidency.[40]

The sectional compromise was nevertheless fragile, as each step in the process of western expansion revealed, because expansion could change the sectional balance of power in the national government. Southern cotton agriculture exhausted the land and required new fields, but it was not land alone that was the main issue for the South, or the North. Northerners were furious when President James Madison, a Virginian, vetoed the bill that would have funded the Erie Canal. In response, a New York congressman introduced an antislavery amendment into the Missouri statehood bill.[41] Nevertheless, a pact was struck with the Missouri Compromise in 1820 that dealt with the expansion of slavery to the territories created by the Louisiana Purchase. The heart of the compromise was to admit Missouri as a slave state, balanced by the admission of Maine as a free state, and to bar slavery in the remainder of the Louisiana territory north of Missouri, or the latitude $36°30'$.[42] "For the time being," says Roger L. Ransom of the Compromise, "the deal that had worked in 1787 had worked again in 1820."[43]

Moreover, the second-party system institutionalized arrangements for sectional compromise with a series of measures that gave the South protection from the voting majorities of the nonslave North. The strategy of balancing the admission of new slave states with new free states, and thus "balancing" representation in the Senate, was complemented by the nomination of "balanced" tickets for president and vice president by the intersectional parties, thus assuring veto power to the slave states.[44] The Democratic Party went further, with a rule that guaranteed substantial representation to the South at their national convention, and a further rule that required a two-thirds vote of the convention for the nomination of their presidential candidate,[45] arrangements that persisted well into the twentieth century.

Sectional conflict flared again in 1846–1847 over the annexation of Texas and the Mexican War, through which the United States acquired some 650,000 square miles of new territory.[46] Northerners were outraged over the tactics the Tyler administration had employed to pry Texas away from Mexico and open it to American slave-grown cotton.[47] They responded with the Wilmot Proviso, an amendment banning African Americans (slave or free) from any territory acquired from Mexico. The amendment failed, but it signaled the growing opposition of the North to the southern thrust for expansion and political power.

A new compromise was struck in 1850, under the leadership of Henry Clay who decried the "intemperance of party spirit," which he attributed to the desire of northern representatives to woo "a small party called Abolitionists."[48] In the new pact, California was admitted as a free state, while other territories would be organized without mention of slavery, slaveholders would be better protected with a new fugitive slave act, and there would be no slave trade in Washington, D.C.[49] "To the militants of the South, as of the North, the Compromise of 1850 was surrender."[50] Neither section was satisfied by the resolution of the conflict over the Mexican territories. Foner quotes an Indiana congressman addressing southern representatives on the question: "It is not room that you are anxious to obtain, but *power— political power.*"[51]

Still, given the enormous costs of dissolution of the Union, why wasn't continuing compromise, although difficult and conflict laden, nevertheless possible? After all, most northerners were not opposed to slavery in the South, and neither were powerful northern interests. True, as the sectional conflict escalated, the South came to be excoriated by northern politicians as the "slave power," but few northerners were preoccupied with slavery. The issues that divided the sections, and made sectional power in the national government so important— high tariffs, a centralized banking system, internal improvements, free land in the west—were susceptible to compromise, as Eric Foner and others have pointed out.[52] Indeed, the history of the Union up to the mid-nineteenth century was a history of more-or-less successful sectional accommodation.

Barrington Moore thinks that the expansion of western commercial farming, which was increasingly tied to the North by its trade relations, is a possible explanation for the growing sectional rift. Moreover, these family farmers feared competition from slavery, just as the South feared independent farming as a threat to their agricultural system. Egnal makes a similar argument, pointing to the growth of the Great Lakes economy and its demand for internal improvements as the root cause of the quarrel.[53] Moore points out that plantation interests in the Senate killed the Homestead Bill of 1852, for example.[54] However, Moore ultimately considers this conflict to have been negotiable, and posits instead as the explanation for civil war the "incompatibilities between two different kinds of civilizations. . . . Labor-repressive agricultural systems, and plantation slavery in particular, are political obstacles to a *particular kind* of capitalism, at a specific historical stage: competitive democratic capitalism we must call it for lack of a more precise term."[55]

But this explanation is not only unsatisfying for its generality, but it also fails to take account of the subsequent accommodation between the sections. After the interruptions of the Civil War and a short-lived Reconstruction, a new sectional compromise was struck that allowed the South to restore its feudal labor system. That compromise lasted until well into the twentieth century. What made sectional agreement impossible in the mid-nineteenth century was the strident and disruptive abolitionist campaign with its demand for immediate emancipation. Abolitionism fractured the institutional arrangements that had undergirded the sectional accord.

The Roots of Abolitionism

As is characteristic of great social movements, abolitionism represented the convergence of different forms of defiance among different groups. Zinn writes of "that mixed crew of editors, orators, run-away slaves, free Negro militants, and gun-toting preachers known as the abolitionists."[56] The interaction of these different groups shaped the course of the movement and contributed to its disruptive power. The polarizing effects of disruption, in turn, fractured the intersectional parties and led to civil war and legal emancipation, the ultimate achievement of the movement. Only when an infuriated South was driven out of the sectional compromise did emancipation become possible.

Abolitionism had multiple and intertwined roots. One set of roots developed in the postrevolutionary period, sparked by the egalitarian ideology of the era, and nourished by the Protestant dissenting faiths. The Quakers were originally especially important.[57] "It would be difficult to exaggerate," writes David Brion Davis, "the central role Quakers played in initiating and sustaining the first antislavery movements." As early as 1774, the Philadelphia Yearly Meeting authorized the expulsion of anyone for buying or transferring slave property, or for serving as executors of estates involving slaves, or for failing to manumit slaves at the earliest opportunity.[58]

Stirred by this theological current, and by the ideas of radical democracy, Pennsylvania, Massachusetts, Vermont, and New Hampshire ended slavery. In the immediate aftermath of the Revolution, abolitionist ideas also spread in the South, or at least in the upper South.[59] But as revolutionary fervor faded, and the invention of the cotton gin made slavery even more profitable and important, the southern system became harsher, including its treatment of free blacks.[60] As for abolitionists, "scores, probably hundreds" of outspoken antislavery whites were harassed into migrating out of the slave South.[61] In any case, if any inclined toward abolition remained in the region, they were silenced.[62]

The religious revival movement that began in the 1820s and swept through New England, and the New England diaspora to the west, reenergized abolitionism.[63] "Evangelical revivalists," says Foner, bred "a commitment to reform the evils they saw in society, and fostered a view of the world in which compromise with sin was sin itself."[64] The revivalists spurred all sorts of reform efforts, including a religious abolitionism that gave the demand for emancipation a new and intense, even fanatical, urgency.[65] In 1831, William Lloyd Garrison founded *The Liberator*, which became the premier publication of the militant abolitionists. Garrison was no gradualist, and he scorned the compromises that a pragmatic political strategy seemed to make necessary. He formulated the demand that became the credo of the militant wing of the movement: immediate and unconditional emancipation. "I *will be* as harsh as truth, and as uncompromising as justice. I do not wish to think, to speak, or write, with moderation. . . . I am in earnest—I will not equivocate—I will not excuse—I will not retreat a single inch—*and I will be heard*."[66]

Abolitionist Disruption

The northern abolitionists were propagandists and proselytizers. They were animated by religious passion and enlightenment fervor, and they believed in the persuasive power of their words. There is no question they were provocative. William Lloyd Garrison burned the Constitution before an audience of thousands at Framingham, Massachusetts, calling it "source and parent of all other atrocities—a covenant with death and an agreement with hell."[67] Inflammatory words aside, mainly they formed antislavery associations, edited papers, and made speeches. By 1841, they claimed 200,000 members in 200 local societies affiliated in

sectional and national associations.[68] Some seventy full-time organizers, called lecturers, were at work, drawn from the ministry, the theological seminaries, and the colleges.[69]

At first glance, none of these activities, considered alone, would
seem to be especially disruptive. After all, the movement's early activity came down to just words. But the words were spoken by people
with deep religious commitment, at a time when a religious revival
movement was sweeping the country, and they were spoken by people
embedded in the Protestant denominations. One of the first signs of
the disruptive potential of the uncompromising demand for immediate emancipation was its impact on the main Protestant churches.[70] The
churches were after all the institutional home of the movement.
Evangelical Protestantism inspired abolitionist ideology, and the churches
also provided both the ministerial vanguard and the social infrastructure that nourished the movement. However, the main Protestant
denominations were intersectional, and the religious ardor that inspired
the abolitionists in the North was mirrored in the South by "Southern
rights" societies that pointed to the Bible as authority for the claim that
slavery fulfilled God's purposes.[71]

Inevitably, antislavery conflict produced schisms in the main
Protestant denominations during the 1830s and 1840s. Methodist con-
vocations had adopted antislavery policies in the 1780s, but opposition
from their congregations made them retreat. The Baptists had been less
tightly organized until the nineteenth century, when the rising conflict
led them to withdraw the freedom they had given their southern con-
gregants.[72] Arguments over slavery split the Methodists into sectional
wings, northern and southern, in 1844, and split the Baptists in 1845.
The Presbyterians were wracked by schism as early as 1837, although
they did not completely divide until 1861.[73] The implications of these
splits for the future, in a nation where religious identities were important in determining political allegiances, were large.[74]

Moreover, uncompromising abolitionist arguments, put forward
righteously in the face of deep race hatred in both the North and the
South, provoked retaliatory fury and violence, both in the North and
the South. Abolitionist meetings were broken up, speakers were
attacked, William Lloyd Garrison was led through the streets of Boston

with a rope around his neck, and Elijah Lovejoy was run out of St. Louis and in 1837 was murdered when a mob in Alton, Illinois, destroyed for the fourth time the press on which he printed his abolitionist paper.[75] Northern abolitionists who ventured into the South faced especially draconian threats from vigilante committees and from state governments as well.[76] "[L]aws ordering the death penalty for abolitionists peppered the statute books of the South," writes Fawn Brodie, and the southern states set ransom prices on the heads of abolitionist leaders.[77]

As abolitionist agitation grew, along with the number of abolitionist societies,[78] the number of antislavery petitions to Congress also increased, urging better enforcement of the ban on the international slave trade, an end to interstate slave trade, or the abolition of slavery in the District of Columbia. Petitions, too, were of course just words, but they infuriated southern representatives. John Calhoun protested that by referring the petitions to committee, Congress recognized their legitimacy: "I cannot see the rights of the Southern people assaulted day after day, by the ignorant fanatics from whom these memorials proceed."

Congress responded with a series of resolutions stating that the body had no authority governing slavery in the states and that it should not interfere with slavery in the District of Columbia, and finally it issued the resolution that became known as the "gag rule," which simply tabled without action all petitions or papers relating to slavery. The gag rule itself then became the focus of controversy, as the abolitionists proceeded to inundate Congress with petitions, until in 1840 the House voted not to receive any antislavery petitions at all. When Joshua Giddings, a Whig representative from Ohio's Western Reserve persisted, he was censured by the House, resigned his seat, and then was triumphantly reelected.[79]

Slave defiance has to be considered part of the abolitionist movement, and in fact it gave the movement much of its disruptive force. Eugene Genovese has argued convincingly that distinctive features of the slave system in the United States, especially the relative dispersal of slave labor and the draconian controls imposed by the slavocracy, made outright black revolt difficult, in comparison to the West Indies and Brazil.[80] The regime of terror in the American South drove black resistance into more covert forms of resistance, into evasion, sabotage, suicide, or running away.[81]

Of course, even episodes of insurrection that occurred elsewhere threw southern planters into a panic, as when, inspired by the French Revolution, Toussaint L'Ouverture led the first successful slave revolution in the world in Haiti in the 1790s, leading to the flight of white planters. Haiti produced as much foreign trade as all the American colonies, and while it belonged to France, the British supplied it with slaves.[82] The revolution ultimately was destroyed with great bloodshed, largely owing to British and French intervention.[83] Southerners were quick to blame the events on misguided white philanthropists, meaning early abolitionists. Subsequent slave revolts in Martinique, Puerto Rico, Cuba, Antigua, Tortola, Barbados, St. Lucia, Grenada, and Dominica did not reassure the South.[84]

Moreover, there were some American slave revolts. In 1800, roughly a thousand slaves gathered under the leadership of Gabriel Prosser to march on Richmond. Their plan to capture the arsenal and take over the city was foiled by bad weather and betrayal, and thirty-five were executed, including Prosser.[85] The South was awash with tales of slave conspiracies, some probably invented, some not. In 1811, four hundred to five hundred slaves rose up on a plantation near New Orleans. They wounded the plantation owner, killed his son, and marched from plantation to plantation recruiting other slaves to the insurrection. The uprising was put down with heavy fatalities by the U.S. army and the militia.[86] In 1817 and 1818, blacks in Florida took up arms with the Seminoles who were fighting to keep their homelands. Teams of blacks and Indians raided plantations, killing whites and carrying off slaves.[87] When Denmark Vesey, a free African American, was put on trial for conspiring in 1822 to lead an insurrectionary plot to burn down the city of Charleston, South Carolina, and spark slave uprisings in the area, northern critics of slavery were again blamed.[88] Nat Turner's rebellion in Virginia in 1831 threw the slaveholding South into a panic yet again.[89] Turner led a band of seventy slaves from one plantation to the other in Southampton, Virginia, killing whites and sparing no one.[90]

The episodes of black rebellion that put fear and rage into the hearts of southern planters had a galvanizing effect on northern abolitionists, most of whom thought their mission was dictated by a higher law than the laws that blacks were violating. The reverse was also true. The rise of abolitionism nourished the hope that made black defiance possible. Southern leaders were probably right to blame the incendiary writing and speeches of abolitionists in the North, by both whites and free blacks, for encouraging black insurgency. Each branch of the movement, in turn, added to its divisive impact on the sectional accord.

In 1829, David Walker, a North Carolina free black who had moved to Boston, published an "Appeal . . . to the Colored Citizens of the World But in Particular and very Expressly to those of the United States," calling on blacks to rise up in revolt. Walker and Garrison were blamed for the Nat Turner insurrection in 1831, which Garrison and his followers had praised. Free blacks in the North, who themselves confronted multiple legal restrictions and intense race prejudice that made them less than free,[91] in turn, helped to provide funds, allies, speakers, and staff for the often beleaguered white abolitionist agitators. Garrison's *Liberator* was funded by money raised by blacks, and Aptheker reports that the subscribers in the early years were overwhelmingly black.[92] Moreover, free blacks had influence with white antislavery leaders, helping to turn them away from African colonization as a solution to American slavery.

What was perhaps the most disruptive strategy of all, the Underground Railway, was a collaborative venture. It was staffed by whites and free blacks who undertook daring undercover exploits, but it was enslaved blacks who made the arduous journeys and risked the brutal punishments meted out to those who were recaptured. To be sure, slaves had run away when they could before, and they had sometimes been helped by sympathetic whites. But the incidence of runaways appeared to be increasing, and the network of help expanding, whether or not it was the systematic project—an underground route with capital, stations, and conductors—that John Hope Franklin describes.[93] Operating in defiant violation of the federal antifugitive laws, the network called the Underground Railway succeeded in bleeding tens of thousands of slaves from the South, further enraging southern slave owners.[94] This was a deadly serious effort. "The only way to make the Fugitive Slave Law a dead letter," said Frederick Douglass, "is to make a half dozen or more dead kidnappers."[95] Governor John A. Quitman of Mississippi declared that between 1810 and 1850, some 100,000 slaves valued at more than $30 million had been helped to escape.[96] Whether his estimate was accurate or not, the sense of threat and anger in the South mounted, deepening sectional tensions.

The penultimate protest before the Civil War, John Brown's daring attempt to seize the federal arsenal at Harper's Ferry, was planned and executed as a collaborative venture, a convergence of black rebellion with abolitionist daring. In the raid itself, five blacks joined with twenty-two whites. The plan was to seize arms in the anticipation that when word of the raid spread, the slaves would rise. The rising did not occur, and the scheme was decried as "the work of a handful of fanatics, led by a lunatic and repudiated by the slaves. . . . [T]he state nevertheless spent $250,000 to punish the invaders, stationed from one to three thousand soldiers in the vicinity and threw the nation into turmoil."[97] And John Brown became an icon to the antislavery North.

Abolitionism and Electoral Dissensus

The abolitionist disruptions inevitably penetrated electoral politics. They injected an intensity into sectional conflicts that made compromise impossible, fragmenting both major parties along sectional lines, and breaking up the sectional compromise. There is little reason to think that this was a deliberate strategy. To the extent that the abolitionists had an electoral strategy—many followers of Garrison believed simply in moral suasion—it was the conventional one of winning converts to influence the outcome of elections. Some abolitionists had entered electoral politics as early as 1840 with the formation of the Liberty Party, parting ways with the zealous Garrison, who feared that an electoral effort would ultimately lead to compromise on the singular goal of immediate emancipation. Running on a single-issue antislavery platform with James Birney, a former slaveholder turned abolitionist, as their candidate, the Liberty Party mounted two presidential campaigns. They peaked in 1844, when they garnered a mere sixty-two thousand votes, although they succeeded in carrying the electoral votes of New York.[98] Horace Greeley reflected on this venture as the Republicans made a bid for the presidency in 1860: "I want to succeed this time, yet I know the country is not Anti-Slavery. It will only swallow a little Anti-Slavery in a great deal of sweetening. An Anti-Slavery man *per se* cannot be elected; but a Tariff, River-and-Harbor, Pacific Railroad, Free-Homestead man *may* succeed *although* he is Anti-Slavery."[99]

In other words, elections are a game won by the parties that mobilize majorities, and the abolitionists clearly could not win. Their success was nevertheless to be registered in their impact on electoral politics, in a context when intersectional alliances were already weakening. In the 1836 vote on the gag rule, northern and southern Democrats voted together, but already the Whigs were splitting on sectional lines.[100] The signs of trouble continued in the instabilities registered in national elections from 1836 to 1852, when no incumbent president could achieve reelection, or even the nomination of his party.[101] In 1844, Van Buren was deprived of the Democratic nomination, which he was widely expected to win, because as president he had opposed the annexation of Texas as a slave state. After Van Buren's southern support fell away, his faction, called Barnburner Democrats, broke with the Hunkers, New York Democrats who supported the administration and refused to endorse the principle of the nonextension of slavery. In 1847, the Barnburners helped organize the Free Soil Party with Van Buren as the presidential nominee.[102]

Van Buren won only 10 percent of the popular vote and did not carry a single state. This signaled to many Democrats that the South had now secured unilateral control of the party.[103] And southern congressmen, provoked by the abolitionists, used their power aggressively.[104] "No proposal was too outrageous" as they tried to make support of expanding slavery a test to impose on northern Democrats.[105] If anything, this broadened the base of the new Free Soil Party. "The southern 'Slave Power,'" writes Kleppner, "was aggressively on the march." Both major parties responded in turn with rhetoric accusing the Liberty Party and Free Soilers of promoting "niggerism" and racial amalgamation.[106] In this political climate, the Compromise of 1850 could not hold.

The swirling currents of sectional conflict inflamed by the abolitionists were disrupting each effort by political leaders at striking a new sectional accord.[107] Moreover, southern anger and aggression only angered and energized the abolitionists, who were still assisting runaways. The new Fugitive Slave Law, which assumed that someone alleged to be a fugitive was in fact a runaway slave unless a hearing, at which the fugitive was forbidden to testify, determined otherwise, was especially provocative.[108] The abolitionists were undeterred. In 1851, a crowd of vigilantes actually rescued a black couple from a U.S. marshal in Boston. The same year, a bloody riot erupted in Lancaster County, Pennsylvania, when the local free black community rose up in arms against a federal posse attempting to enforce the act.[109] These events did not restrain the slaveholders who launched massive manhunts, seizing even blacks who had lived free for years. During the first fifteen months that the Fugitive Slave Law was in force, eighty-four alleged fugitives were returned South by federal commissioners, and only five were released. Over the decade, 332 blacks were sent into slavery, and only 11 were released.[110]

The Know-Nothings, otherwise known as the American Party, entered the electoral lists in the early 1850s. Their roots were in a clandestine nativist fraternal society, the Order of United Americans, and their leaders included prominent conservative Whigs. Their doctrinal pronouncements were preoccupied with the decline in social order, which they attributed to the influx of Irish immigrants, who they castigated not only for their poverty, but for their dissolute lifestyle, their radicalism, and their fierce loyalty to a presumably conspiratorial Roman Catholic Church. But the Know-Nothings were also antislavery, inheriting the Whig view that the South was anachronistic and inefficient compared to free-labor capitalism. In 1852, the Whig national convention denied the nomination to the conservative favorite, President Millard Fillmore, and turned to antislavery candidate Winfield Scott. The Whig vote in the South evaporated, and the party virtually collapsed.[111] Conservative Whigs in the North threw in with the Know-Nothings.

In 1854, Stephen Douglas led the effort to push through the Kansas-Nebraska Act, which would give settlers in those new states the right to decide for themselves whether to be slave or free. Because the act overturned the 1820 Missouri Compromise, reaction in the north was explosive, and something like a guerilla war was precipitated as proslavery and free-soil forces rushed into Kansas to swing the outcome. There is not much reason to think that the free-soil guerilla bands in the fight were mobilized by the quest for black emancipation. Indeed, the free-soilers later wrote a constitution prohibiting free blacks from entering the state.[112] More likely it was, as Moore says, a fight over different economic systems, animated for white settlers by the fear of competition from slave labor rather than by abolitionism. But the abolitionist participants helped bring the conflict to a fever pitch. John Brown's raid on proslavery settlers in Kansas, followed by the retaliatory and bloody attack on Lawrence, an antislavery stronghold in the state, "electrified the North" and gave the emerging Republican Party "an almost invincible combination of issues. . . . Northern fury was intense, widespread, and of immense political significance."[113]

It was in the midst of these events that the Republican Party entered the contest for national power, more or less as a single issue party powered by the question of slavery, or rather the question of the extension of slavery raised by the Kansas-Nebraska Act. State-level Republican parties formed during 1854 and 1855, and convened in 1856 to form a national party and nominate a presidential ticket. Sundquist sums up the state-level Republican activity: "Throughout the 1854–56 period, state Republican conventions 'deliberately avoided by common consent' all issues other than slavery. . . . Slavery, said Senator [Charles] Sumner, 'is the only subject within the field of national politics which excites any real interest.' "[114]

The new party nominated a popular hero, Colonel John C. Fremont, as their presidential candidate, and added a few planks dealing with a central railroad to the Pacific and with river and harbor improvements, issues with strong appeal in the North,[115] to their Kansas-Nebraska preoccupation. The heart of their platform, however, was their assertion of congressional authority over slavery in the territories, and the demand for the immediate admission of Kansas as a free state.[116] "Free Soil, Free Labor, Free Men, Fremont," was the chant at Republican rallies. Meanwhile, the Democrats had nominated James Buchanan, who upheld the Compromise of 1850 and the Kansas-Nebraska Act, and called for noninterference by Congress with slavery in the states and territories, or in the District of Columbia.

The Republican Party campaigned in the context of rising anger and excitement about the virtual war in Kansas between free-state and slave-state settlers. The caning on the Senate floor of Senator Sumner also stirred northern indignation. In November 1856, the Republicans entered what became a three-way contest in the north. The Know-Nothings had nominated Millard Fillmore, a former Whig who had signed the Fugitive Slave Act. Fillmore inherited some of what was left of the Whig vote but carried only 12.6 percent of the free-state electorate. Democratic candidate Buchanan carried 41.8 percent of the northern vote, down eight percentage points from the Democratic total only four years earlier in a similar three-way contest. Republican candidate Fremont carried eleven northern states and 45.6 percent of the northern vote, and this just two years after the party had formed. Since Buchanan carried every slave state except Maryland, he won the election.[117] It was clear, however, that the longstanding southern fear of northern electoral power could be realized. If the Republicans could recruit Know-Nothing voters in the North, they would be able to elect the next president.

The merger began in Pennsylvania in 1857, when Republicans and some Know-Nothing leaders joined together to form a Union Party that absorbed most of the Know-Nothings. The Union Party was short-lived, but it bridged the transition of the Know-Nothings to the Republicans. The pattern was followed elsewhere, and by 1860 most of the Know-Nothings had joined with the Republicans. The party also gained support from the Panic of 1857, which Republicans blamed on the low-tariff policies of the Democrats.[118] Then the Supreme Court, with a southern majority, issued the Dred Scott decision, ruling that slavery could not be prohibited in the territories, and declaring the Missouri Compromise unconstitutional.[119]

The Dred Scott decision struck down the Compromise of 1820 on the grounds that Congress had no power to deprive a slaveholder who moved into a new territory of his property. Its immediate effect was to tamp down the Kansas wars.[120] But in 1859, John Brown's raid on Harper's Ferry and his subsequent hanging added another martyr to the abolitionist cause, stoking southern fears of a black rebellion on the one hand, and of a Republican in the White House on the other.

Southern extremists had been talking about the creation of their own republic for years, but now the cause of disunion gathered momentum, especially within the Democratic Party. A party convention in Charleston broke up when Cotton Belt delegates walked out over the failure to adopt a plank demanding a federal slave code for the territories. The Democrats entered the race of 1860 shattered. The northern wing nominated Stephen Douglas; the delegates who had bolted backed John C. Breckenridge of Kentucky; and others joined with former Whigs to back still another new party, the Constitutional Union party, which chose John Bell of Tennessee as its candidate.[121]

But by 1860, Democratic disunion did not matter. Lincoln won the election by 180 votes to 123 for his three rivals taken together, on a broad platform that called for the nonextension of slavery and condemned threats of disunion as contemplated treason. Reflecting the range of sectional interests that had pulled together to form the new party, the platform also called for river and harbor improvements, a homestead act, the protective tariff, and a Pacific railroad.

The South was not reassured by Lincoln's moderation on the slavery issue. Seven southern states responded to Lincoln's victory by adopting ordinances of secession.[122] By the time the president took office, the new Confederacy had attacked Fort Sumter, which Lincoln moved promptly to defend, and civil war began. Four more slave states then seceded.

The Republicans had not carried Congress. The secession of the southern states, however, yielded the Republicans overwhelming majorities in the Congress which they used to legislate their sectional economic agenda, passing the Homestead, Land Grant College, and Pacific Railway acts, and increasing tariffs within four years to a spectacular average of 47 percent.[123]

At the outset, Lincoln tried hard to avoid the inflammatory issue of emancipation. The war, he said, was to preserve the Union. But as the war wore on, the exigencies of an indecisive campaign, and perhaps also the passions excited by the terrible bloodshed, drove Lincoln toward emancipation. The insurrectionary role of the slaves themselves was probably critical to his decision. The South relied on black slave labor. But during the war, hundreds of thousands of slaves refused to work and deserted the plantations, crippling the Confederacy's ability to feed itself or its army. At first, blacks who rushed to help the Union Army were turned away. But as the war wore on, Union commanders pushing into the South welcomed the tide of blacks offering their services. Some 200,000 ultimately joined the Union Army and took high casualties, and, together with the tacit strike of black slave laborers, they probably turned the tide of war, giving victory to the North.[124] When, after much hesitation and a number of compromise proposals, Lincoln issued the proclamation that emancipated the slaves in the rebellious states, Lincoln cast his action as militarily necessary to suppress the rebellion.[125]

War and southern secession had also given the abolitionist cause momentum. Even before the war ended, Congress passed the Thirteenth Amendment banning slavery, and the states remaining in the Union ratified it. Then, in late spring of 1866, Congress adopted the Fourteenth Amendment, along with the Civil Rights Act of 1866. When the white electorate in southern states refused to ratify the Fourteenth Amendment, sometimes violently, Congress resolved on "military reconstruction," federal troops were deployed and southern states were permitted to reenter the Union only after they enfranchised blacks and ratified the amendment. The efforts of southerners to prevent black voting continued, now by means of private paramilitary units like the newly formed Ku Klux Klan. In response, Congress passed the Fifteenth Amendment to forbid racial discrimination in voting, and it was ratified in 1870.[126]

The abolitionists had triumphed. And they had done so through a strategy that relied on electoral politics, even while scorning the normal rules for electoral influence. Perhaps strategy is not the right word. After all, there is no evidence that abolitionists intended by their persistent agitation and disruption to drive wedges so deep into the sectional alliance as to split the major parties. Still, that is what they did, and that is why they won.

Of course, legal emancipation was a limited victory. Still, with emancipation achieved, the abolitionist movement melted into the Republican Party, where they continued to lobby for a variety of measures to improve the circumstances of the freed but totally impoverished former slaves. But they were no longer a disruptive force, and in any case, the electoral context had completely changed. Southern and northern political leaders struck a new accommodation, eliminating the fissures that had earlier given the abolitionists electoral influence. With the sectional accord restored, southern elites moved rapidly to restore their control over black workers, using an array of stratagems from legal codes requiring that blacks accept employment, to mass incarceration, to disenfranchisement. These efforts, which began immediately after the war, were only briefly interrupted by Reconstruction policies.

Nevertheless, even a partial victory that tempered the condition of the most crushed and abused people in the country, in the face of overwhelming opposition, deserves acknowledgment, analysis, and respect.

FIVE

Movements and Reform in the American Twentieth Century

IN THIS CHAPTER I discuss the politics underlying the major egalitarian reforms that occurred in the 1930s and 1960s. Much of the
work I have done over the past decades in collaboration with
Richard Cloward has been devoted to analyzing these episodes.[1] We
have emphasized the important role of disruptive protests in precipitating twentieth-century waves of democratic reform. This chapter will
build on this earlier analysis. First, I will summarize our argument and
briefly indicate the kind of evidence to which we pointed. Second, I
turn to a review of some of the voluminous academic literature that
also purports to explain policy breakthroughs that occurred between
the 1930s and 1960s, resulting in the creation of what is sometimes
called the New Deal/Great Society order. The pride of place that
Cloward and I give to protest movements puts us at odds with most of
this academic work, which pays rather scant attention to protest movements. I will argue that, important insights notwithstanding, the mar-
ginalization of protest in this literature has produced interpretations of
the political dynamics of these periods that are sorely incomplete.

Finally, I turn to another and older line of academic argument that
points to shifts in electoral politics to explain the bursts of new policy
that occurred in the 1930s and 1960s. This literature also ignores the
role of disruptive threats. Yet by emphasizing shifts in electoral coalitions, it provides a foundation for analyzing the process through which
the disruptive power of movements was translated into policy reform.

The short shrift given to protest by contemporary political studies is the more surprising because much of this literature was produced in the wake of a new and celebrated brand of historical scholarship that came to be known as "history from below." With the British Marxists in the lead, historians in the post–World War II period directed attention to the political actions of ordinary people, of workers and peasants and the urban poor. They insisted that the role of the lower strata in politics had been overlooked, in part because of the unwarranted assumption that crowd actions like food riots or the pulling down of the houses of their well-off enemies, were not politics. To understand history from below, they argued, the scope of inquiry had to be broadened to include the distinctive forms of often unruly political action of people lower in the social order. Nor could it be assumed that the riotous crowd was ineffectual in shaping state policy. To the contrary, analysts such as Eric Hobsbawm, E. P. Thompson, George Rudé, Raymond Williams, Charles Tilly, and a host of American labor historians sifted the evidence to assess the influence on state policies of the claims made by "history from below." The Tillys summed up the main point: "Homely forms of collective action . . . were the principal means by which aggrieved and inspired groups of ordinary people shaped the European structure of power."[2] However appealing such declarations, the "history from below" analysts have had little influence on the academic literature on contemporary policy development.

This work did influence the study of social movements, however. Where once movements were regarded as exotic eruptions, we now think of them as forms of purposive political action, or, as Tilly says, "a set of people who . . . commit themselves to a shared identity, a unified belief, a common program, and a collective struggle to realize that program."[3] In other words, contemporary movement analysts declare their subject to be a form of politics. Nevertheless, contemporary movement studies pay relatively little attention to the impact of protest on policy, or to the complex dynamics through which this impact is realized. Instead, the focus is mainly on movements as sociological phenomena: their precipitants, their internal dynamics and organizational forms, and the mechanisms of movement recruitment and socialization. This conclusion was drawn by McAdam, McCarthy, and Zald in a survey article on collective protest prepared for Neil Smelser's 1988 *Handbook of Sociology*: "The interest of many scholars in social movements stems from their belief that movements represent an important force for social change . . . . Rarely, however, have movement scholars sought to assess how effective movements are in achieving their ends."[4] Others have repeated the point since.[5] In 1995, Burstein, Einwohner, and Hollander asserted that "the field of social movements grew tremendously in the 1970s and 1980s, but the study of movement outcomes did not."[6] And in 1999, Amenta, Halfmann, and Young made the point again, that "far more research addresses mobilization than impacts."[7]

If movements are regarded as a form of politics, the question of outcomes ought to be crucial, for it is outcomes that ultimately measure the power of the movement, as a number of social movement analysts have indeed recognized.[8] Nevertheless, despite the respect now accorded history from below, and despite some notable efforts to focus specifically on outcomes, work tracing the impact of protest movements on policy remains thin and without much influence on our understanding of American political development.[9] In consequence, schools of thought that privilege other actors, and other forms of power than disruption, still dominate our interpretations of American politics.

Before I proceed to the argument of this chapter, I need to comment on the relative absence of protest-influenced reform in the long historical space that intervened between the abolitionists and the New Deal. After all, nearly six decades passed between the end of reconstruction and the "big bangs" of reform of the twentieth century. Moreover, there was a good deal of popular unrest during these intervening decades, as the country rapidly industrialized and corporate monopolies grew, fueled in part by federal policies that promoted capital formation, railroad development, and high tariffs. Rapid growth also led to intense competition and exceptional economic instability; deep and frequent downturns meant unemployment, wage cuts, and hardship. Not surprisingly, there was protest. Workers facing wage cuts during the severe depressions that marked the 1870s, 1880s, and 1890s erupted in great strikes and riots. Local, state, and federal political officials responded not with concessions, however, but with police, militia, and federal troops.

Farmer protests did not fare much better. The populist movement during the late nineteenth century arose among farmers squeezed by high-cost credit, falling agricultural prices and high railroad and granary rates. Not only did the farmers want relief from tight credit, high railroad rates, and low commodity prices in a pattern than echoed the English chartists, but they recognized that concentrated wealth was corrupting political democracy. When they came together in Omaha in 1892 to form a National People's Party, they called for a progressive income tax, the direct election of senators, the secret ballot, and the eight-hour workday. Those reforms would not be won for a long while, and when they were, it was not in response to the protests of the populist farmers.[10]

The failure of these movements to secure any political relief was almost surely not because they were insufficiently disruptive. The great railroad strikes of 1877 set off waves of rioting, arson, and looting that extended from Pittsburgh to Chicago, and to many smaller towns that the railroad reached. Tens of thousands of workers attacked company property and the police, and thousands of railroad cars were destroyed, as were roundhouses and other buildings. And the strikers had considerable mass sympathy, particularly in Pittsburgh, the center of the conflagration.[11] The Pullman Strike during the spring of 1894 precipitated a nationwide boycott of all trains carrying Pullman sleeping cars, paralyzing the major lines in the west and hampering railroad transportation everywhere. But the very scale of the disruption proved to be an excuse for the use of federal troops to smash the strike, and it led to the jailing of Eugene Debs and other strike leaders. In these and other incidents, the death tolls inflicted on the insurgents were horrific, and labor actions continued to be met with violence well into the twentieth century.[12]

Perhaps the failure of these late nineteenth-century protests to produce significant reform was owed to the fact that the protests did not threaten the electoral fragmentation that had been key to the victory of the abolitionists. As Elizabeth Sanders says, local protest actions had been the preferred strategy of the American Federation of Labor before 1906, and of the Farmer's Alliance as well.[13] But after the defeat of the mass strikes of the late nineteenth century, many of the leading activists, particularly among the socialists who often led the mass strikes, and among the populist farmers as well, concentrated their efforts not on disruption and its fragmenting effects, but on the normal electoral activity through which they hoped to build a party to promote their program. The socialists worked, with some inspiring success on the local level, to build an alternative party.[14] The populists, after experimenting with third-party initiatives, formed a fatal alliance with the Democrats in the election of 1896. True, Williams Jennings Bryan, the fusion candidate, lost only narrowly, but he lost by a larger margin than other losers in the closely contested presidential races of the late nineteenth century. Meanwhile, the Republicans under the leadership of Mark Hanna successfully mobilized big business into national politics. Hanna, Kevin Phillips says, "all but tithed Wall Street and the manufacturing community"; some businesses actually notified workers not to show up if Bryan won.[15]

There are undoubtedly other factors than their failure to mount a serious electoral challenge that account for the defeat of the late nineteenth-century protests. The ethno-cultural issues that dominated the popular appeals of the major parties blocked the sharp emergence of the economic issues that the protest movements were trumpeting. Then, also, the corruption of elected officials by corporate, railroad, and mining money was so far advanced that voter disaffection mattered less. State legislatures and state courts were for sale, and state legislatures in turn controlled the Senate, and therefore the federal bench. The entire governmental system seemed to have become virtually immune from popular claims.[16] Even when reform proposals succeeded in the state legislature, they were struck down by the state courts. Or measures that found some response in the House died in the Senate, during a period that Kevin Phillips describes as the Senate's three-decade corporate captivity. Or they were overturned by the court. "[D]emocracy," says Phillips of this period, "was corrupted at its constitutional core."[17]

Explaining the Big Bangs

Almost all of the labor, civil rights, and social welfare legislation of consequence in the industrial era was enacted in just two six-year periods: 1933–1938 and 1963–1968 (with the exception of the Supplemental

Security Income program of 1972, a delayed federal reaction to the state and local fiscal burdens resulting from the great expansion of the relief rolls in the 1960s).[18] Largely as a result of these legislative initiatives, federal authority and spending expanded (at the expense of both private actors and subnational authorities), and much of this new authority and spending was oriented toward a measure of economic redistribution and toward measures to democratize some American institutions.

Thus, during the first big bang, national income support programs were initiated, at first in the form of emergency relief, which reached millions of people and supported them at levels that amazed and often outraged local elites.[19] The Civil Works Administration work relief program created during the emergency winter of 1933–1934 went so far as to eliminate the means test and pay wages far more generous than the average relief benefit. Together, relief and work relief programs reached 28 million people, or 22.2 percent of the population,[20] and social spending increased rapidly, from 1.34 percent of the Gross National Product (GNP) in fiscal 1932 to 5 percent by 1934. In 1935, the Social Security Act established the framework for almost all of our income support programs, beginning with old age pensions; unemployment benefits; and "categorical" programs for the uncovered aged, the blind, and orphans, the programs that came to be known as "welfare." Subsidized housing programs were introduced for the first time. By 1938, the level of social spending in the United States approximated that of the leading European welfare states.[21]

The 1960s saw the major expansion of most of the entitlements inaugurated in the 1930s, including the liberalization of old age pensions and unemployment insurance through extension of coverage and higher benefits; a quadrupling of the numbers of women and children on the Aid to Dependent Children program; the creation of Medicare for the elderly and Medicaid for the poor; and new nutritional programs, of which the food stamp program was most important, since it expanded from only forty-nine thousand monthly participants in 1961 to over 11 million by 1972.[22] The Elementary and Secondary School Act of 1965 provided federal aid to education targeted especially to poorer school districts, and new subsidized housing programs were initiated, as was the Model Cities Act of 1966, which provided funds for inner-city development. Overall, federal expenditures in support of individual and family income increased from $37 billion to $140 billion in the decade after 1965. By the mid-1970s, official poverty levels had dropped to an all-time low, from 20 percent in 1965, to 11 percent.[23] Federal spending was projected to reach $373 billion in fiscal 1982. Together with matching funds contributed by states and localities for Aid to Families with Dependent Children (AFDC) and Medicaid, projected to reach $25 billion, these sums were equal to 12 percent of the estimated GNP.[24]

Political rights expanded in each period as well. The extraordinary mass strikes that began in 1934 finally produced the National Labor Relations Act of 1935 which not only enunciated the right of workers to organize for collective bargaining—that had occurred before—but also created an enforcement mechanism for that right in the National Labor Relations Board, and gave some legal protections to strike actions.[25] As David Plotke says of the National Labor Relations Act, "[I]t was sharply discontinuous with prior practices, though elements of its approach were prefigured in Woodrow Wilson's administration and in the NRA."[26] In 1938, the Fair Labor Standards Act established national minimum wages and maximum hours. These provisions were the basis for the development of a culture of rights among unionized workers that made possible huge advances in their circumstances over the next three decades.[27]

In 1964, at the peak of the civil rights movement, the Twenty-Fourth Amendment to the Constitution was passed, striking down the use of the poll tax in federal elections. This, together with the Civil Rights Act of 1964 and the Voting Rights Act of 1965, overrode the state and county restrictions on the franchise that had been put in place by southern states after Reconstruction. And once the electoral system of the South was opened to blacks, the system of southern apartheid collapsed, with far-reaching consequences that virtually toppled southern caste arrangements. In other words, the black movement of the 1960s finally won, a century later, the reforms first announced in the Fourteenth and Fifteenth Amendments. Meanwhile, the Equal Opportunity Act of 1964 (the antipoverty program) even fostered the use of federal funds by poor communities, especially by minority communities, to organize to press municipal government for more services and patronage. Many African American mayors and congressional representatives got their start in the antipoverty community action programs.

So, why these big bangs in policy development? The clustering of major policy initiatives coincided exactly with the clustering of episodes of mass disruption, with the mobilization of interdependent power from below, and in a range of institutional arenas. The economic downturn of the 1930s and the hardships that ensued rapidly brought the mob, or "the people out-of-doors," to life. Bands of people descended on markets and delivery trucks to demand or commandeer food. Irving Bernstein concludes that in the early years of the Depression, "organized looting of food was a nation-wide phenomenon."[28] Rent strikes spread, and crowds formed to block evictions for nonpayment of rent. The actions began to take a more explicitly political form too, with the spread of unemployed demonstrations and marches demanding relief in the early 1930s. Veterans marched on Washington with a similar demand for early payment of the bonus due them for service in World War I. Farmers spilled their milk and formed crowds that threatened sheriffs to prevent foreclosure sales.[29]

The first response of the federal government after the election of 1932 was the creation of a system of emergency relief, but then relief centers became the target of protesters, demanding immediate attention to their grievances.[30] Then, in 1934, industrial strikes began. The first big action was the "Battle of Toledo," in which the unemployed joined in support of striking workers. Worker protests escalated with the general strikes that followed in Minneapolis and San Francisco and in the southern textile industry. Strikes became larger; there were 17 strikes of 10,000 or more in 1933, 18 in 1934, and 26 in 1937 when 1,860,000 workers walked out.[31] Fifteen strikers were known to have been killed in 1933, and forty more in 1934. In a period of eighteen months, troops were called out to cope with strikers in sixteen states.[32] Strikes continued to increase in 1935 and 1936; and in 1937, when the Supreme Court ruled on the constitutionality of the National Labor Relations Act, strikes reached their highest level in the twentieth century.[33]

Disruptive protest, this time by African Americans on the one side and the white southern "movement of massive resistance" on the other side, came to a head again in the mid-1960s. During the spring of 1963, the civil disobedience campaigns in Birmingham, Alabama, used the full panoply of civil rights tactics, from sit-ins to boycotts to demonstrations that launched thousands of children into the streets to face mass arrests and police who unleashed teeth-snapping guard dogs and rib-crushing high-pressure water hoses against the demonstrators. By May, organized protests were giving way to rioting, forcing local business leaders to call for a truce, and the federal government to intervene. That summer, a march "for jobs and freedom" sponsored by the main civil rights organizations attracted the largest number of demonstrators that had come to Washington up to that time. But the march only signified the nationalization of the movement, as in its aftermath, rioting spread to virtually every major city in the country between 1964 and 1968.

In short, the surge and ebbing of disruptive protest events defined the beginning and ending of social policy bangs. Of course, correlations do not establish causes. We need to know about the political process that leads to new policy initiatives, and whether disruptive protest plays a consequential role in that process. In fact, the major policy interpretations that attempt to explain the big bangs of the 1930s and 1960s avoid this question, choosing to ignore or marginalize protest in favor of other explanations, with the consequence that there remains a black hole in their causal logic.

Historical-Institutionalist Explanations

The currently most influential interpretation of twentieth-century policy reform in the United States is offered by historical-institutionalists. The school originated two decades ago as a so-called state-centered school, focused mainly on criticizing the economic determinism of the neo-Marxist explanations of American policy that were popular at the time.[34] It has evolved since then to include the study of the influence of political institutions on political processes more broadly, and has also variously renamed itself as "institutional politics" or "polity-centered."[35]

Historical-institutionalists who focus on twentieth-century social policy initiatives often begin by pointing out that the late emergence of

American social policies, together with the explosive pattern of their development, requires a theoretical departure from an older and influential explanation often called "the logic of industrialism." This older theory, usually justified by pointing to the evolution of European welfare states, attributes the development of modern social policies to the new social needs generated by economic growth, and to the enlarged state fiscal capacities generated by growth. Moreover, as industrialization advanced, so did electoral-representative political arrangements that made the growing working class a potent constituency for these policy initiatives to enhance economic security. The influence of this logic of industrialism perspective has been considerable, for it seems to explain the broadly parallel expansion of welfare state programs across the West. It also became the template for the introduction of analyses that attempted to explain country differences within that broad trend, by variously placing more emphasis on culture, on class conflict, or on the political exigencies that shaped the emergence of class-based electoral coalitions.

The questions that preoccupy historical-institutional scholars who undertake to explain the New Deal/Great Society order belong to this latter intellectual development: Why, when the United States was not a laggard in either industrial or political development, was it a laggard in welfare state development?[36] And why, when the logic of industrialism suggested a gradualist development of policy, was the pattern of American policy development so explosive, with most welfare state policies initiatives concentrated in either the mid-1930s or the mid-1960s?[37]

To explain the laggard American welfare state, the historical-institutionalists point to unique constraints that limited the growth of social policy initiatives. Thus they argue that a distinctive American "policy heritage" and the more limited capacities of our national government explain why, for example, World War II led to broad national social welfare reforms in Great Britain, but only to fragmented programs in the United States.[38] Similarly, much attention is devoted to the inhibiting effects on new initiatives of the federal system in the United States. The constraining influence of subnational authorities on federal initiatives presumably explains why, for example, the implementation of unemployment benefits was ceded to the states. Other limits on new social policy initiatives were generated by distinctive American electoral arrangements, including a party system that relied on patronage, thus making elites fearful of the potential abuses of social policy. Then also constitutional and congressional arrangements privileged a southern congressional delegation determined to prevent federal policies that would interfere with the southern system and especially with its low wage and chattel labor.

These more specific elaborations notwithstanding, the overall point of view is clear. Institutional arrangements that developed at one point in time, in response to a particular configuration of political interests, limited the options available at subsequent political junctures. The phrase used to capture this idea is "path-dependence." As Weir says, "One of the most powerful factors determining how groups define their policy interests and which alliance they enter is the organization of political institutions."[39] Orren and Skowronek state the idea most clearly: "Different historically evolved configurations of interest politics and state power within each country . . . determine paths—national trajectories—along which alternatives for change in the future are limited by changes in the past."[40]

There is ample evidence of institutional constraints, and surely they are part of the answer to why the United States was a social policy laggard. However, and perhaps inevitably, a theoretical toolkit dominated by inherited institutional limits fares far less well in explaining periods of explosive change.[41] If features of American political institutions inhibited policy development, those features were nevertheless at least partly overridden during the big bangs of social policy creation. And once initiated, new policies obviously change institutional arrangements. The big bangs led to enormous growth in national government capacity as a result of the enlargement of its policy and spending authority. None of this could easily have been predicted as a simple outgrowth of earlier policies.

For example, much is made by the historical-institutionalists of the impediments to national initiatives posed by preexisting state and local policy authority. At first glance, the federal emergency relief program of 1933 seems to provide evidence of the influence of this state-centered constraint. Relief had always been a state and county responsibility, and the new national emergency relief program was designed, in principle, to conform with that precedent. Responsibility for operating the programs was delegated to the states and counties, and they were required to contribute three dollars for every one dollar from Washington. So, institutional precedents mattered, somewhat. But many states wouldn't or couldn't allocate the funds, and political conditions in 1933 made it imperative for the Roosevelt administration to field a mass relief program rapidly. Insurgency by the unemployed, in the form of rallies, riots, rent strikes, looting, and takeovers of local and private relief offices, was mounting, and strapped and beseiged local officials were clamoring for help. So the federal money poured out, whether or not state governments paid their share. Indeed, national officials simply federalized the administration of relief in six resistant states.[42]

A further example that reveals the force of the political imperative of responding to insurgency rather than the influence of institutional precedents can be seen in the rather heavy hand with which the national administration ran the Works Project Administration (WPA) and the Public Works Administration (PWA) programs. Even the design of the unemployment insurance program broke with institutional precedents far more dramatically than it bent to them. Only Wisconsin had established an unemployment insurance program, although as the Social Security Act neared enactment, four other states initiated programs.[43] And although the program was to be implemented by the states, it was to be funded by a federal payroll tax, the proceeds of which were to be returned to states that legislated their own programs. Potentially recalcitrant states were thus left with the choice of either going along or having the federal government run the program instead. In these and other instances, there is, to be sure, evidence of the influence of institutional impediments, but there is also evidence that these impediments were sometimes overcome. Clearly, something else, and something big, was also going on.

Or consider the big bang of the 1960s. A marked feature of a number of the new national programs was that they broke with the grant-in-aid formula devised in the 1930s. Under this formula, federal funds were disbursed to state or local governments for specific programs, with states and localities required to contribute substantial matching funds.

But as in the 1930s, the new programs of the 1960s were launched with considerable urgency, and only nominal contributions from state or local governments were required. Indeed, the lower levels of the federal system were often bypassed in favor of a host of other intermediaries, many of them new organizations created in the central city ghettos specifically to receive the funds. Weir acknowledges that the reliance on local "community action agencies" in the poverty program was a "striking departure," which she explains not by reference to her institutionalist model, but by the haste with which the program was launched, and the way its loose structure allowed different perspectives and innovative ideas to create niches within the executive branch.[44]

But this explanation is less than satisfactory, particularly since the design was reiterated in program after program—from juvenile delinquency, to mental health, to the community action component of the poverty program, to model cities—and this despite the mounting objections from local officials who felt their powers were being usurped. To be sure, a complete untangling of this story also reveals the large and persisting influence of the preexisting structure of intergovernmental relations, since much of the new money did indeed go to traditional municipal agencies in the by-then customary form of grants-in-aid. Some of the money, however, not only bypassed these agencies, but was even used to organize political pressure on old-line municipal agencies to shift benefits and services to minority communities.

The something else that explains the specific shape of these new initiatives was the massive movement of the black insurgency that was spreading across the country. Rising black demands in turn sparked sharp conflicts with the white working class, and with big city Democratic administrations. These troubles in the urban strongholds of the Democratic Party were made more acute because they occurred at a time when the southern base of the party was crumbling. The "striking departure" of community action was an effort to manage urban racial conflict while holding urban voter loyalties. This was done with strategies not very different from the clientelist methods through which ethnic conflicts had been contained and voter loyalties secured in the past. Antipoverty community action agencies looked very much like the storefront offices of the big-city political machines, doling out some services, some jobs, a good deal of rhetorical support, and intervening with municipal and state agencies to get people more benefits.[45]

The Supplemental Security Income (SSI) program provides another important example of the overriding of institutional constraints. Notwithstanding the policy precedents of state and local control of categorical relief programs for the indigent elderly, blind, and disabled, all of these programs were placed under the Social Security Administration in 1972. The question is why, against all precedent, the federal government made itself responsible for administering means-tested programs. The answer, I think, is that the black insurgency in the cities, much of it animated by grievances over unemployment and extreme poverty, had forced a huge expansion of the welfare rolls, and state and local officials were themselves clamoring for a federal takeover as a way of easing fiscal and political pressures. Congress had a choice of relieving local fiscal strains by federalizing AFDC or by federalizing relief programs for the elderly and disabled. The Congress chose the latter less contentious course, but the contribution of welfare protests in creating the political preconditions for this major policy innovation should not be ignored.

More generally, here's the rub. Analysts of institutional constraints on policy development are left with no way to explain the appearance of new social policies during the big bangs, policies that at least partly overrode constraints. This is why Edwin Amenta, who relies on the full battery of state-centered explanations to explain why the United States was a welfare laggard, nevertheless reverts to an electoral argument to explain the rapid expansion of welfare policy in the 1930s. He argues that during the Depression, there were more "pro-spenders" in Congress. True. But why did congressional representatives become pro-spenders in the 1930s? What happened that led voters and politicians to break with the fiscal conservatism of American politics? An institutional explanation is surely incomplete without taking into account electoral developments. And electoral changes in turn were at least in part propelled by the protest movements, which raised issues and threatened electoral instability.

None of this is to deny that the constraints the historical institutionalists point to must be part of an adequately complicated model.

Still, references in their arguments to factors which might explain how institutional precedents were overcome are passed over quickly, and certainly are not theorized. Orloff refers to "popular pressures" in accounting for the New Deal breakthroughs only to brush them aside as less important than the factors favored by state-centered theorists.[46] Skocpol also tries to diminish the role of protest in New Deal initiatives, acknowledging only that the "new welfare regime" of the 1930s was a response to "democratic ferment."[47] Just what this means remains puzzling, since she is at such pains to diminish the role of labor protests in New Deal labor initiatives. She acknowledges a growing strike wave, and then says, "It cannot plausibly be argued that these strikes directly produced the Wagner Act of 1935. . . . The U.S. industrial working class was not strong enough to force concessions through economic disruption alone.[48] Since to my knowledge, no one—and certainly not Piven and Cloward, whom she cites—has argued that disruption made itself felt outside the context of a complex and unstable political environment, it is hard to know what to make of this.

Skocpol also acknowledges that in the 1960s "blacks were pressing the federal government and the Democratic party" to expand social programs for the poor, but this process remains peripheral to her analysis.[49] Similarly, Weir tells us that the southern civil rights movement and urban riots in the mid-1960s were "contingent factors" that heightened the political profile of employment policy, but then the "upheaval in racial politics" of the 1960s is not only dismissed as a cause of the war on poverty but is blamed as the reason that the war was aborted.[50] Comments such as these are efforts to fill the black hole that remains when movements and their electoral impact are ignored. The theoretical moral that is drawn highlights inherited institutional impediments or boundaries, and not the popular political forces which sometimes swamp them. As Sheingate puts the point in an argument with the institutionalists, the political world "is also dynamic and subject to periodic events such as new social movements, unexpected electoral outcomes, or dramatic policy initiatives that institutional approaches predicated on stability cannot easily account for. . . . Our knowledge of structure-induced stability has come at the expense of understanding the very struggles and conflicts at the center of political life."[51]

Reform Ideas

Another line of argument, sometimes joined with historical-institutionalist accounts, explains American policy initiatives by pointing to the influence of the ideas of particular reformers or reform organizations, or, in a newer vernacular, to the policy discourse that reformers promoted. In other words, they point to professed do-gooders and experts as the engine of reform.

There are numerous examples. Long before American political scientists became interested in explaining social policy, this sort of explanation flourished in the field of social work, which embraced the nineteenth- and early twentieth-century view that social progress was the achievement of moralizing philanthropists like Jacob Riis, Jane Adams, or Robert Hunter.[52] Theda Skocpol actually makes a similar claim when she says that it was in large part the maternalist vision of the women's organizations of the early twentieth century that made them effective in launching the short-lived social policies of that period.[53]

This kind of argument recurs in histories of the 1930s. Plotke thinks that "in formulating and passing the Wagner Act, the leading agent was a progressive liberal political leadership."[54] The ideas of "progressive liberals" about reordering labor relations were the main (but Plotke does not think the sole) force behind the Wagner Act.[55] Similarly, James T. Patterson seems to think that the increase in welfare spending and the development of social insurance in the 1930s was owed importantly to the efforts of reform organizations like the National Federation of Settlements, the American Public Welfare Association, and the American Association of Social Workers, and to the efforts of specific reform-minded individuals such as Ewan Clague, I. M. Rubinow, and Edwin Witte.[56] And since reformers often work hand-in-hand with politicians and bureaucrats, or indeed become politicians or bureaucrats, an emphasis on the role of reformers easily morphs into the historical-institutionalist perspective.[57] Thus Skocpol and Ikenberry argue that the initiative for Social Security legislation was owed to New Deal officials and the reform groups and policy intellectuals with whom they were allied.[58]

A similar emphasis on reformers emerges in histories of 1960s policies, and blends easily with state-centered arguments, especially since many of the reformers were in fact government officials and, indeed, presidents. John F. Kennedy is widely said to have been moved to push new initiatives on poverty by the misery he saw when he campaigned in West Virginia in 1960. Lyndon Baines Johnson is said to have pursued Kennedy's initiatives out of nostalgia for his youthful associations with the New Deal. Experts doubling as reformers are often said to have been influential in the design of the Great Society programs, as when Daniel Patrick Moynihan criticizes "those policy-oriented professionals who came to power" in these years.[59] He particularly singles out Richard A. Cloward and Lloyd E. Ohlin, academic consultants to the President's Committee on Juvenile Delinquency and Youth Crime, and blames them for drawing up the community action blueprint that influenced many of the Great Society programs and that created so much political controversy, especially in the big-city wing of the Democratic Party.

Margaret Weir also thinks the ideas of experts were a major influence on employment and social policies in the 1960s.[60] She blames the failure of the federal government to address structural labor market issues in the 1960s on the reformer experts associated with the Council of Economic Advisers whose mistaken emphasis on the problems of individuals influenced the design of the program.[61] And Alice O'Connor, in a book devoted specifically to the role of social scientists and policy experts in 1960s poverty policy initiatives, also attributes a large role to the Kennedy administration Council of Economic Advisers, and particularly to experts who believed in human capital theory and so promoted education and training programs as the key to social mobility among the poor.[62]

All of this happened. There were reform organizations and reformers, and they were active in the circles in which policies were being fashioned, and perhaps their ideas mattered in fashioning reform policies. But there are usually reform organizations and reformers, and they always try to influence policy, most of the time without much success. The problem is obvious: these reformers had ideas, to be sure, but settlement house leaders, social workers, and policy experts by themselves have little political clout. They are not credible as forces accounting for far-reaching policy initiatives that upset established arrangements between levels of government and between government and markets, and that cost lots of money besides.

A singular focus on reformers and their moral commitments and policy ideas begs the question of who it was or what it was that opened the door for particular reformers and invited them into the councils of government, and just which reformers were singled out to be invited in. Something else was going on. William Gamson's research provides empirical data that casts light on the something else. Gamson studies fifty-three claims-making organizations that arose between 1800 and 1950, and tries to identify the factors that account for their relative success or failure. Referring specifically to the 1930s, he makes the point that challenging organizations of long standing were more successful than those that formed during periods of turmoil. But his data also show that those organizations, many of which can reasonably be considered reform organizations, won what they won during what he calls "turbulent periods," characterized by "social unrest" and "general crisis."[63]

Power Elite Theories

Another interpretation of the politics that led to reform in the mid-twentieth century sees the new policies as the accomplishment of powerful economic interest groups, sometimes acting in their own name, but often acting through reformer surrogates. This "power elite" school—a close kin to the "corporate liberal" school popular a couple of decades ago—provides a more persuasive answer to the question of who or what promoted the new policies, and why they succeeded. In this view, reformers are influential not because they have new ideas or because they are experts, but because they are surrogates for business elites. The underlying argument is that economic elites are the prime movers in politics, and in reform politics as well.[64] Initiatives attributed to early twentieth-century "municipal reformers," for example, were reanalyzed by adherents of the corporate liberal school as the political efforts of businessmen in reformer guise.[65] Similarly, while groups such as the American Association for Labor Legislation (AALL), the Business Advisory Committee (BAC), and the Presidential Advisory Committee on Economic Security (CES) are treated as organizations of reformer experts by some analysts,[66] they are treated as part of a policy network linked to corporate leaders by others.[67]

The view that corporate leaders were the main reformers has been very influential in studies of New Deal social insurance legislation. Colin Gordon and, more recently, Peter Swenson provide good examples.[68] Gordon traces corporate support for the pension and unemployment insurance provisions of the Social Security Act to earlier "welfare capitalist" initiatives that held the prospect of "reducing labor turnover and increasing the interest of the employees in the success of the company as a whole."[69] Gordon argues that the uneven implementation of the resulting plans, as well as the inconsistent policies of the states that took up the reforms, helps to account for why business interests came to support a national system of pensions and unemployment insurance under the Social Security Act. And the "reformers" who carried the ball, such as the American Association for Social Security, and key legislators like Robert LaFollette of Wisconsin or Robert Wagner of New York, "served merely as articulate voices for the regulatory programs of industries and firms."[70]

Similarly, Swenson sees business as the dynamic force in the New Deal. He quotes J. Douglas Brown, a corporate-friendly industrial relations expert, who said in his 1935 Senate testimony that Social Security "protects the more liberal employer" and "levels up the cost of old-age protection on both the progressive and unprogressive employer."[71] However, Swenson says, their historic antigovernment ideology led the business community to delegate the task of initiating the legislation they wanted to reformers.[72]

Because power elite theorists believe that business interests are ordinarily dominant and in a position to promote the policies that serve their interests, they need to explain the abrupt pattern of policy formation that characterized the 1930s and 1960s, and also the multiclass benefits of the resulting policies. While the emphasis is usually on problems and fissures among capitalists, trouble from below is also sometimes invoked as an explanation. Thus Quadagno emphasizes divisions between monopoly and competitive capitalists in the shaping of Social Security legislation, but she also acknowledges the pressures generated by Depression-era movements that made the legislation imperative.[73]

Ferguson develops a scheme in which the level of class conflict, under-stood as labor conflict, actually determines the party alignments of cap-italist class fractions.[74] Domhoff defines his methodological approach straightforwardly as searching out "the institutional affiliations of lead-ers within the upper class, corporate community, and policy-planning network to determine what seem to be the primary power-elite orga-nizations . . . [and to] then study the policy positions of those organi-zations." To be sure, social movements are a kind of contextual element in his arguments, for they cause the "general disruption in the social structure" to which the power-elite responds.[75] Colin Gordon also acknowledges that the Social Security Act was "spurred in large part by reform and class pressures in the trough of a depression."[76] And Peter Swenson sees the experience of labor militancy, fueled by the excesses of skinflint employers, as spurring industrialists to support negotiated agreements with unions in the mid-1930s.[77]

Still, this doesn't seem quite good enough. Some power elite theo-rists acknowledge a role for protest movements as a contextual factor, but disruptive movements are not treated as causal forces that deserve to be the focus of theory. Hacker and Pierson in fact make this point in their critique of Swenson. Their argument is that even business leaders who supported Social Security, and they do not think there were many, acted in a political context that had already greatly circumscribed their choices.

> [E]mployers faced a political situation in which some options (such as inaction or a set of publicly overseen private codes of conduct) were no longer on the table, while others pushed by populist forces that sought ends most business leaders feared were. . . . With Democrats holding huge margins in Congress, the Depression wors-ening, and populist challenges mounting, employers were pressed to choose among a set of more or less interventionist government responses.[78]

This brings me to a consideration of interpretations that empha-size electoral forces, and the interplay of electoral and disruptive poli-tics in the policy initiatives of the 1930s.

Electoral Shifts or Realignments

The current popularity of the historical-institutionalist perspective notwithstanding, the most influential explanation of twentieth-century policy change probably remains the interplay between electoral shifts and political leaders. The big bangs are interpreted as "big electoral bangs." Kevin Phillips waxes romantic about what he calls the "star-spangled singularity" of American politics, which permits "bloodless revolutions" through critical presidential elections that produce "revolutionary changes in the nation's political culture and economic development."[79]

How do such electoral upheavals occur? There are two hypotheses in the literature, and although they are often treated as alternatives, there is evidence for both of them. First, there is the mobilization thesis. Referring to the 1930s, Degler, Lubell, Converse, Miller and Stokes, and Andersen, for example, say that hard times together with Democratic appeals raised the level of turnout in the growing pool of immigrants and their children who had become eligible to vote.[80] In the alternative "conversion" thesis, economic depression and widening hardship pried existing voters loose from their traditional attachment to the Republican Party, as was argued early by V. O. Key in his theory of "critical elections."[81] Similarly, E. E. Schattschneider associates the "profound change in the agenda of American politics" that occurred during the New Deal with the change in voter and party alignments. Sundquist also finds an urban and class-based shift of voters at the heart of the New Deal program.[82] Burnham, whose work on critical realignments is greatly influenced by Key and especially by Schattschneider, also attributes the "reorganization" of national policy to electoral shifts at the "grass roots" (the impact of which he thinks are increasingly limited, however, by "the onward march of party decomposition").[83] Burnham explains the relationship:

> Voter and party realignments, arise from emergent tensions in society which, not adequately controlled by the organization or outputs of party politics as usual, escalate to a flash point; they are issue-oriented phenomena [that] . . . result in significant transformations in the general shape of policy.[84]

And Ginsberg provides broad empirical confirmation of the correlation of voter shifts and policy change for most of the nineteenth and twentieth centuries.[85]

Or, in a somewhat more complex but nevertheless similar analysis, Richard Bensel attributes New Deal policy initiatives to a sequence of developments in which economic crisis and political confusion, by paralyzing the metropolitan-industrial elite, left entreprenurial Democratic Party leaders free to promulgate the policies leading to the bipolar New Deal majority coalition between the northern working class and southern agrarian elites.[86]

For some purposes, the dispute between "mobilization" and "conversion" interpretations may be important (and certainly it is important to the strategists of successive electoral campaigns, as demonstrated in the fierce debates between those who call for attracting "swing" voters and those who call for mobilizing "the base"). If the mobilization analysts are right, new voters are the key to realignment; if the conversion analysts are right, changing party loyalties among existing voters are the key. Either way, or both ways, however, the interaction between voters activated by hard times, whether old voters or new or both, and political leaders striving to win or hold their support is said to have led to the policies that were oriented toward relief and economic recovery, and that first created and then stabilized the New Deal coalition.[87]

Dissensus Politics

I agree that electoral politics plays a large role in an explanation of the big bangs. In contrast to theories that emphasize institutional constraints, the role of reform ideas, or even business interests, electoral analysts point to new and distinct political forces to explain new and distinct policies. Moreover, they point to forces of sufficient magnitude to constitute a credible explanation for major policy shifts. Still, electoral explanations by themselves ultimately founder on their circumscribed view of politics. For these analysts, the political world is populated mainly by voters, and by the party leaders who respond to them.[88] The interaction between politicians and voters is said to generate policy innovation, particularly at times when an externally induced crisis like economic collapse unsettles old patterns of voter allegiance. V. O. Key captures the reasoning when he says, referring to electoral data from the 1930s, that:

> [V]oters are not fools. To be sure, many individual voters act in odd ways indeed; yet in the large the electorate behaves about as rationally and responsibly as we should expect, given the clarity of the alternatives presented to it and the character of the information available to it. . . . [T]he portrait . . . [is] of an electorate moved by concern about central and relevant questions of public policy, of government performance, and of executive personality.[89]

And presumably, an electorate moved by central and relevant questions of public policy in turn moves politicians.

But this is altogether too simple a view of American electoral politics. Voters may not be fools, but neither are atomized voters capable, by themselves, of asserting new policy demands. And politicians in a two-party system do not easily play that role either. The reasons are straightforward. Even putting aside the corrupting role of money and organized interest groups, politicians seeking to win office need broad majorities, especially in a winner-take-all two-party system. And to build and hold those broad majorities, they try to avoid conflict, searching instead for the safe and consensual appeals to family, prosperity, and flag that will preserve and enlarge voter coalitions. Even the party out of power, left to itself, tends to be timid in a two-party system, if only because the minority party is never entirely out of power, especially when the government the party strives to control is decentralized and fragmented.

Indeed, when electoral shifts do occur, they are not automatically followed by bold new policy initiatives, no matter the campaign rhetoric. Roosevelt and the Democratic Party won the 1932 election with an undifferentiated majority that drew from all sections and all income groups. True, FDR's inflammatory campaign rhetoric denounced economic royalists, but his party's platform merely reiterated the main planks of the 1920s. He did not call for emergency relief. Something else brought relief and work relief, to the top of the policy agenda.

Something else made agricultural credits, first demanded by the populists at the end of the nineteenth century, an imperative in 1933. Similarly, FDR and most congressional Democrats were largely indifferent to labor policy. As Plotke points out, organized labor claimed a puny 10 percent of the nonagricultural labor force in 1930, and its influence within the Democratic Party was slight.[90] To be sure, the Democrats nominally supported the right to organize, but not government enforcement of that right. Something else happened to make FDR reverse himself and, together with the Democratic Congress, support the National Labor Relations Act of 1935. The something else was the rise of protest movements and the institutional disorder they threatened.

Protest movements raise the conflictual issues that party leaders avoid, and temporarily shatter the conservative tendencies of two-party politics. Indeed, conflict is the very heartbeat of social movements. The urgency, solidarity, and militancy that conflict generates lends movements distinctive capacities as political communicators. At least for a brief time, marches and rallies, strikes and shutdowns, can break the monopoly on political discourse otherwise held by politicians and the mass media. Where politicians seek to narrow the parameters of political discussion, of the range of issues that are properly considered political problems and of the sorts of remedies available, movements can expand the political universe by bringing entirely new issues to the fore and by forcing new remedies into consideration.

This dynamic has exactly the consequences that political leaders in a two-party system fear. By raising new and divisive issues, movements galvanize groups of voters, some in support, others in opposition. In other words, protest movements threaten to cleave the majority coalitions that politicians assiduously try to hold together. It is in order to avoid the ensuing defections, or to win back the defectors, that politicians initiate new public policies. The prospect or reality of voter dissensus is the main source of movement influence on public policy. This is the "something else" that is missing in dominant accounts of public policy development in the United States.

The causal chains that connect movements to policy reforms can be traced to the impact of collective defiance and the institutional breakdowns that ensue on electoral coalitions. By the time FDR took office, escalating insurgency among the unemployed, along with the pleas of alarm from frightened mayors and local elites exposed to their protests, brought relief and work relief to the top of Roosevelt's policy agenda. Similarly, farmer protests in the context of a still-fluid New Deal majority prompted the passage of the Agricultural Adjustment Act of 1933. And only as the Roosevelt administration's halfway measures to conciliate striking workers backfired, enraging industrialists and workers alike and causing strikes to spread, did FDR reverse himself and back the National Labor Relations Act of 1935, which put government authority behind the right to organize.

Jenkins and Brent make a similar argument about the interplay of protests, electoral alignments, and elite competition on the Social Security Act of 1935.[91] The sustained protests of the unemployed, farmers, the aged, and especially workers not only fed off each other but also generated increasing voter volatility. In working-class areas, voter turnout increased. Meanwhile, third-party challengers emerged, including the End Poverty in California initiative; the Non-Partisan League and other farmer parties in the Midwest; and, most importantly, the Huey Long challenge which brought together the Townsend movement, Long's Share our Wealth Society, and Father Coughlin's National Union for Social Justice. Roosevelt called on Frances Perkins to head the CES in the spring of 1935 with these words: "We must not delay. I am convinced. We must have a program by next winter and it must be in operation before many more months have passed."[92]

The sense of crisis among political leaders was intense. As the 1936 election approached and the protests of the aged spread, FDR introduced the Social Security Act, a multitiered and complexly shaped effort to respond to both the aged and their numerous supporters among the electorate, and to limit the emergency relief program ceded earlier in response to the insurgent unemployed.

Electoral analysis alone provides an even less persuasive analysis of the Great Society than it does of the New Deal. For one thing, analysts cannot cite general economic collapse as the catalyst of shifts in voter allegiance. Instead, Sundquist too breezily describes the politics and policies of the 1960s as evidence of "aftershocks" of the New Deal realignment. Other analysts point to the 1964 election, in which the massive Goldwater defeat was accompanied by an equally massive defeat of the Republicans in Congress. The newly enlarged Democratic congressional majorities then proceeded to enact the policies that together came to be known as "the Great Society."[93] But while the enlarged Democratic majority now had the capacity to enact new policies, its sudden willingness to push through radically new initiatives still has to be explained.

The confluence of influences on the second big bang was complex. The peculiar and fragile majority coalition which came to underpin the New Deal Democratic Party rested on the support of the Bourbon South and the working-class urban North. The fragility of this coalition was aggravated by the economic modernization of the South and the resulting displacement of many southern rural blacks. Released from plantation bondage, they migrated to the cities, where their concentrated numbers and the fact that growing numbers were now wage-workers and voters yielded them new resources for influence. The rise of the civil rights movement and later the explosion of urban black protests reflected these developments and also contributed to emerging cleavages in the Democratic Party.[94] The point I want to underline here is that the Democratic leaders who finally ceded civil rights legislation and social policy reforms were not responding simply to voter preferences (or to institutional precedents, or to the influence of reformers), but to voters who were being activated by the protests first of the civil rights movement in the South, and then by black protests in the northern cities.

Thus, civil rights protests in the South where most blacks could not vote nevertheless had electoral effects. Early protests had signaled the new risk by spurring the defection of urban blacks from the Democratic Party; black Democratic voting fell from 80 percent in 1952 to 60 percent in 1956. Black turnout in the northern cities fell as well. Meanwhile, white southerners enraged by black demands mobilized in a movement of "massive resistance" led by southern politicians, who were also Democrats. In 1960, John F. Kennedy managed to win back some black votes with renewed promises of action on civil rights, but true to the practice of leaders in a two-party political system, he hedged on new initiatives once he took office, fearful of southern defections. It took the clear evidence that the white South was defecting from Democratic columns despite his efforts at conciliation, together with the rising militancy of the civil rights movement, and signs that civil rights protests were spreading to the Democratic strongholds in the urban North, to force his hand. By 1963, Kennedy finally sent major civil rights legislation to the Congress, and the first of the Great Society social policy initiatives as well. After Kennedy's assassination, Lyndon Johnson stayed the course, with the Civil Rights Act of 1964 and the Voting Rights Act of 1965, and the battery of Great Society legislative initiatives of the mid-1960s.

In fact, as protest movements escalate, the conflictual issues they raise penetrate the parties from within as well as pressing them from without. Movement activists become party activists and, at least temporarily, the usual two-party calculus of holding and building majorities by avoiding conflictual issues may be overridden by the need to appease these activists within the party.[95] Thus Democratic leaders in the 1960s and 1970s had to contend not only with the problem of building majorities in the face of intense public conflict, but with the problem of holding the party together, or at least holding the campaign organization together, in the face of polarizing demands by the cadres of party workers attracted by the party's commitment to civil rights or to environmental, antiwar, or women's issues. In much the same way, the influence of the pro-life and New Right movements of the 1980s and 1990s penetrated the Republican Party, and forced conflict-generating appeals onto the Republican agenda, with ultimate consequences that are still unfolding.[96]

It hardly needs saying that the results of internal and external conflict in the 1960s and 1970s were costly to the Democrats. Nevertheless, an array of new policy initiatives had been won, with enormous consequences for African Americans and for the American poor generally. Moreover, the insurgent spirit of these movements, the electoral instability that they both reflected and to which they contributed, and the victories they won helped inspire other movements, among women, the disabled, and gays and lesbians, for example.

Movements subside. And when they do, other political interests reemerge and gain traction, including political interests that draw their support from the unease and opposition generated by the movements themselves. Still, these disappointments are not grounds for denying the protest movements their achievements.

CHAPTER
SIX
꙲

The Times-In-Between

ISRUPTIVE MOVEMENTS are relatively short-lived. They
burst forth, often quite suddenly and surprisingly, and after a few
years, they subside. Ruling groups are at first unsure that the crisis has passed and they only slowly reconnoiter. When the path seems
clear, they begin to mount the political initiatives that lead to the rollback
of at least some of the gains yielded by protest. The stunning reforms
won by the abolitionists, culminating in the Thirteenth, Fourteenth,
and Fifteenth Amendments to the Constitution, were eviscerated by
new state constitutions that stripped blacks of the vote, by state legislation that institutionalized a system of apartheid, and by state and local
regimes that relied on mob terror to enforce the near-total social and
economic subordination of blacks.

Labor victories in the mid-1930s were first chipped away by subsequent legislation, and were then further weakened by the administrative decisions of an increasingly business-friendly National Labor
Relations Board. The social welfare programs begun in the 1930s lan-
guished after the Depression until a new period of protest forced their
expansion in the 1960s. Within a decade, the rollback of those social
programs became the aim of Republican and business crusaders who
first targeted the Great Society programs and welfare, and then turned
their sights on Social Security, the big program begun in the mid-1930s.
If analysis of the moments of reform in American history reveals the
important role of disruptive protest movements, so does the analysis
of the periods in which these reforms are whittled back reveal the

weakness of electoral arrangements as an avenue for democratic reform in the absence of disruptive protest.

But why does disruption subside? The answer is that the processes set in motion by the protest movement alter the political conditions that once encouraged defiance. The movement also changes, partly in response to these changing conditions, and partly because the internal dynamics of the movement make disruptive political action hard to sustain. I pause for a moment to expand on these points.

There is a sort of common sense about the decline of movements that is in fact illuminating. One familiar idea is that protest movements subside simply from a kind of exhaustion. I think there is truth in this. The eruption of protest is usually exhilarating to the protesters, as people revel in the discovery or rediscovery of their interdependent power, of their ability to "shut it down," and also their experience of the sense of strength that comes from mass action. But exhilaration does not last forever. Moreover, defiance entails costs, the costs of suspending the relations on which the protesters also depend, and sometimes the cost of repression as well. Strikers at the very least lose their wages, and sometimes they also risk the exit of the businesses that are the targets of their action. Factory managers, for example, may simply terminate the employment relationship by firing strikers or by closing plants and relocating elsewhere. Serious disruptions have to contend with the threat or actuality of physical force, wielded by company police, hostile mobs, or by government authorities who often single out more militant protesters for punishment. People who occupy facilities or block streets may be hauled off to jail, and rioters may simply be gunned down. Repression of course works to temper the willingness of masses of people to risk disruptive action. Pressures come from all sides in the multiple relations in which people are embedded to restore normal daily life.

The other commonsense theme is that protest subsides when the protesters "win," when they achieve some amelioration of their grievances. In all of the cases I have examined, concessions were made to the movements. But as I have argued elsewhere with Richard Cloward, these conciliatory responses are always less than what the movement had demanded.[1]

Why, then, would not partial victory embolden and energize the disruptors? The answer is that concessions are rarely unencumbered. They are usually accompanied by measures to reintegrate the movement or its leaders into normal politics, as leading abolitionists were absorbed into the Republican Party; as labor leaders and their organizations became tethered to relationships with factory management and the Democratic Party; and as civil rights activists were absorbed into local, state, and national electoral politics, whether as mayors, state legislators, congressional representatives, or as bureaucrats.

Moreover, the movement wins what it wins because it threatens to create or widen divisions in electoral coalitions, because it makes enemies, and activates allies. The threat of dissensus has inevitable limits, however. On the one side, the mere fact of concessions, even limited concessions, tends to rob the movement of its erstwhile allies. After all, grievances have been answered, so what more do these people want? On the other side, once opponents have actually been driven out of the coalition, the fatal threat is no longer available. The party may succeed in regrouping as a dominant party no longer vulnerable to the threat of dissensus, as the Republican Party did after the Civil War, and as the Democratic Party did after the 1930s. Or it may survive, albeit in a weakened state, as the Democratic Party did after the civil rights movement cost it the support of the South.

All this said, my point in this chapter is not to analyze the dynamics of movement decline. Rather I want to bolster the evidence I have presented for my argument that disruptive movements are responsible for the truly brilliant moments of reform in American history by showing that when the movements decline, there are few new reforms, and those won at the peak of movement power are often rolled back.

Efforts to contain radical democracy during the revolutionary period began almost at once with the rewriting of state constitutions. Once the war was won, elites sought to further curb democratic gains in the new Constitution, a process I described in chapter 3. Still, the uncertainty of elites trying to gain their footing in the new polity coalesced with the still-vigorous belief in democracy to lead to an expansion of the franchise. Property qualifications that had restricted voting before the revolution were steadily lowered in the first decades of the nineteenth century, and more officials were required to stand for popular election, including governors, presidential electors, and many local government officials. Voter participation among white men surged, reaching 80 percent of the eligible electorate by 1840.[2]

In fact, these new spheres of democratic and even exuberant participation proved manageable through two sorts of arrangements. The first arrangement was presaged in the writing of the Constitution and the creation of a national government. Its essential feature was to wall off from electoral influence those parts of government that performed functions essential to a commercial economy. The second set of arrangements was the result of the development of new techniques for organizing mass electoral participation.

The fervor of the radical democrats reflected their belief that participation in government would yield them influence over the conditions bearing on their own and their community's well-being, and not least over their economic well-being, as the rush of some of the states to issue cheap money, or to relieve debtors, revealed. As I argued in chapter 3, the design of a national government was a defense against these democratic political currents. Officeholders in the new national government were shielded from direct voter influence by the arrangements for the indirect election of the Senate and the president, and by the establishment of an unelected Supreme Court. A national government designed to be insulated from popular influence was given authority over an array of policies critical to propertied elites, including currency, taxation and spending, and the maintenance of a navy and standing army that would protect overseas commerce and large landholdings in the west. Toward the same commercial ends, the states were specifically prohibited from enacting laws creating trade barriers or impairing the obligations of contract.

These constitutionally dictated arrangements were significant because they meant that important policies were decided by a government geographically remote from the local communities where people lived and worked and organized, and made more remote by the indirect system of elections specified in the Constitution. The interests of bankers were secured from state-issued cheap money, the power to tax and spend meant that the rich men who held bonds issued by the wartime Continental Congress, which the states had been reluctant to redeem, would be repaid; and new tariffs were imposed to protect American manufacturers from European competition.

Over the course of the nineteenth century, the national government continued to play a large role in American economic development, financing the infrastructure of canals in the first half of the nineteenth century, and later subsidizing (many times over) the construction of a national railway system. Late nineteenth-century efforts by a number of state governments to regulate the railroads were nullified by the Supreme Court. And as industrial capitalism grew, the Court issued interpretations of labor rights rooted in the "master-servant" tradition of English common law, declared unions to be conspiracies, and later ruled unions to be a violation of antitrust law, even while it shielded corporations from state government efforts at regulation by ruling that these corporate entities were individuals protected under the Fourteenth Amendment.

The institutional arrangements that allowed these government policies were justified because they were embedded in the basic legal structure of the nation. Of course, the Constitution changed over time, but the process of changing the Constitution was itself specified in the Constitution. Amendments were difficult and cumbersome, and extremely unlikely to succeed in the face of organized opposition. As for change through judicial interpretation, that depended on a Court that was itself shielded from electoral influence by the lifetime appointments of the justices.

It would be a mistake, however, to conclude that it was mainly governmental centralization that foiled democracy in the nineteenth century. To be sure, many business-oriented policies were centralized. But even while some policies were centralized, other policies less critical to the propertied, or less likely to be disputed, were decentralized, an arrangement also embedded in the Constitution. Indeed, the United States has been distinctive among Western democracies for the vigor of its decentralized levels of government, and that vigor resulted from the fact that these subnational governments did indeed do many things that bore directly on the lives of ordinary people. They raised school and property taxes, administered schools and other local services, and policed the streets. The localization of these sorts of public activities contributed to a lively and intense local politics and made possible the distinctive techniques for mobilizing and controlling mass electoral participation that developed in the United States.

Of course, in a vast and diverse nation, with only a primitive communication and transportation infrastructure, business-oriented policies were also promulgated at the state and local level. Indeed, the legal framework that defines the responsibilities and the liabilities of the corporation was a creation of state law. And states and localities were responsible for much of the public infrastructure that not only made community life possible, but on which commerce and manufacturing depended, and which also constituted vast opportunities for business profit. The notorious corruption of local and state politics in the nineteenth century owed much to these opportunities for profit and the political patronage they yielded. So, state and local governments not only did things that mattered, but they yielded the patronage resources on which the clientelist politics that distinguished the American nineteenth century were built. The fabled popular electoral politics of the nineteenth century became a carnival of both mass participation and massive corruption, and participation and corruption were closely interbraided.

To be sure, many of the accounts of nineteenth-century machine politics are folkloric and appealing. Local politics is depicted as pageantry, with marching bands, rallies, hoarsely shouted slogans, and genial pot-bellied political bosses. "There was no spectacle, no contest, in America that could match an election campaign," writes Richard McCormick, "and all could identify with and participate in it."[3] Tocqueville is the oft-cited authority:

> No sooner do you set foot on American soil than you find yourself in a sort of tumult. . . . A thousand voices heard at once. . . . One group of citizens assembles for the sole object of announcing that they disapprove of the government's course, while others unite to proclaim that the men in office are the fathers of the country. . . . It is hard to explain the place filled by political concerns in the life of an

American. To take a hand in the government of society and to talk about it is his most important business and, so to say, the only pleasure he knows.[4]

Such depictions fasten on the surface manifestations of popular politics and do not probe the terms on which high levels of voter participation were mobilized.

Democracy arrived early in the United States, at a time when group formation and collective identity were mainly communal and church-based. By contrast, in Western Europe the franchise was not won until the turn of the twentieth century, when industrialization was well-advanced and both unions and the working-class political parties that fostered class-based identities had already developed. In the nineteenth-century United States, communal and church attachments were strong, and class identities were still weak, allowing the leaders of the emerging mass parties to develop strategies for recruiting voters and holding their allegiances that were relatively nonthreatening to the interests of party elites and the business groups that were allied with the parties. Ethno-religious identities were especially important as the basis for voter mobilization,[5] as Tocqueville, who visited the United States at a time when revival movements were sweeping the country, emphasized. "Religion," he said of Americans, "should be considered the first of their political institutions."[6] The strength of the churches, and the proliferation of church-related voluntary associations, joined religious crusading to partisan fervor. Later in the nineteenth century, rapid immigration and labor-market competition also fueled the fractious ethnic tribal politics that characterized electoral politics.

Clientelism supplemented tribalism as a strategy of voter management. As voter participation expanded in the first decades of the nineteenth century, so did the uses of government patronage to build the organizations that could develop and maintain clientelist relations with the enlarging electorate. Generally speaking, this mode of voter organization and control appears to thrive in situations where formal enfranchisement precedes the modes of self-organization of working people that the spread of mass-production industries encourages. Southern Italy and Mexico are twentieth-century examples that come quickly to mind. In other words, in the absence of trade unions, worker fraternal associations, and working-class parties, voters more easily became prey to party operatives supported by patronage, who enlisted votes on the basis of tribal identities and in exchange for personalized goods, service and friendship.[7]

In sum, the victories won by the mobs of the revolutionary era under the banner of radical democracy became the basis of a system of political incorporation that substantially eliminated the threat that radical democracy had once posed. The outer forms of elections and representation remained and even expanded, but the idea that democratic participation would yield the people control over the state, and that this control would force the state to respond to the people's interests, especially their economic interests, had been subverted.

Or consider the losses suffered by the cause of emancipation once the abolitionist movement subsided. The achievements of the movement are undeniable. The boldness and single-mindedness of the abolitionists shook and divided the major Protestant denominations, fragmented the intersectional parties of the third-party system, and drove the infuriated southern states to secession. With the influence of southern representatives removed, the national government launched a war to preserve the Union, emancipated the slaves, and then at the war's end passed the Thirteenth, Fourteenth, and Fifteenth Amendments to the Constitution.

These achievements were contested, although the searing experience of the Civil War offered protection for the reforms for a time. When the armies laid down their arms, the southern states quickly tried to regain control of their black labor force. State laws were enacted which limited the areas in which the freed slaves could rent or purchase property, and stiff vagrancy laws forced them to work on the employer's terms, as did laws which effectively prohibited blacks from quitting employment on grounds of breach of contract.[8] When the white electorate of the southern states refused to ratify the Fourteenth Amendment, which was understood at the time as empowering the national government to enforce the Bill of Rights against both the states and against individuals,[9] provoked Republicans in the Congress responded by ordering the deployment of federal troops across the South, and allowed southern states to rejoin the Union only if their constitutions granted blacks the vote and if the states ratified the Fourteenth Amendment. In 1871, President Grant used federal troops to crack down on the new Klan in South Carolina, and federal courts convicted hundreds of Klansman in the early 1870s of violating the freedmen's new rights.[10] These policies almost surely owed more to the antisouthernism that the bloody Civil War had generated in the North, than to deep support for emancipation. Paul Kleppner makes exactly this point: "Republicans knew, and the state referenda continued to inform them, that there was little mass support for black suffrage." But black suffrage "had become inextricably bound together in their belief systems with an antisouthernism seared into consciousness by the war experience . . . and . . . hostility to the party of treason."[11]

Congress quickly used the new powers granted by the new constitutional amendments to pass legislation reinforcing the political rights of the freedmen, and also, with the Civil Rights Act of 1866, guaranteeing the freed slaves "the same right in every state and territory of the United States, to make and enforce contracts, to sue, be parties, and give evidence, to inherit, purchase, sell and convey real and personal property as is enjoyed by white citizens."[12] When President Andrew Johnson vetoed the Civil Rights Act of 1866, as well as several bills to create and enlarge the Freedmen's Bureau, Congress overrode the vetoes, and by comfortable margins. Other laws to protect the civil rights of blacks followed quickly. In 1875, Congress went so far as to ban segregation in public accommodations, transportation, and entertainment facilities, and only filibusters prevented Congress from banning segregation in schools.[13] Federal troops and federal policy in turn made possible the remarkable local and state-level initiatives that marked the brief flowering of reform in the period called Reconstruction.

By the mid-1870s, the tide of reform was receding. After the disputed election of 1876, federal troops were withdrawn from the secessionist states, and the period known as Redemption began. As the abolitionist movement dissipated, and its influence in the Republican Party declined, the influence of railroads, banks, and industrialists grew. The federal policies that had made the Reconstruction era possible were of little concern to the business interests that now dominated the Republican Party. Indeed, those interests, especially the railroads, had rapidly acquired important stakes in the New South. The old planter class had been destroyed, but a new class of more capitalist planters had taken its place, many of them northerners or supported by northern money.[14] And new methods of coercing black labor emerged, including convict leasing and sharecropping.

Still, the racial order of the South remained undecided for a time. The constitutional amendments that had spelled "A New Birth of Freedom,"[15] along with the Civil Rights Act of 1866, remained the law of the land. And although trickery and mob violence were reducing their voting numbers, blacks were still enfranchised and still voted in large numbers, and black officials were still being elected.[16] Indeed, when the Populist movement emerged in the 1880s among white farmers hard pressed by agrarian depression and the lien system through which they were losing their land, the Populists competed with conservatives in the Democratic Party for the votes of the freedmen.[17]

Meanwhile, however, the rollback of the achievements of abolitionism and the Civil War continued. The Supreme Court issued a series of decisions that effectively nullified the restrictive parts of the Civil Rights Act, and also ruled that the Fourteenth Amendment gave Congress the power to restrain the states, but not individuals, thus smoothing the way legally for the restoration of near-total white racial domination in the South. The Federal Elections Bill of 1890 was the last national effort to protect black voters. It failed in Congress, and most southern Republicans faded into the Democratic Party. After the Supreme Court decision in the *Plessy v. Ferguson* case in 1896, the restored white supremacist order was firmly based not only in southern state and local governments, but in the three branches of the national government as well.[18]

The crucial rollback over the longer run occurred through the disenfranchisement of blacks, effectively reversing the Fifteenth Amendment.[19] Mississippi was the pioneer in 1890 of methods for black disenfranchisement that evaded the constitutional guarantee of the right to vote, by imposing property tests, literacy qualifications, poll taxes, the requirement that only those who had served in the Civil War could vote, felon disenfranchisement laws, and good character clauses, all made effective by a system of voter registration staffed by local election officials determined to prevent blacks from voting.[20] South Carolina followed suit in 1895, Louisiana in 1898, North Carolina in 1900, Alabama in 1901, Virginia in 1902, Georgia in 1908, and Oklahoma in 1910.[21]

Once blacks were virtually eliminated from the electorate, mob lynchings escalated and Jim Crow laws multiplied, unimpeded by the need of state and local officials for black votes. The path was thus smoothed for the unfolding of the postbellum southern system of total economic and social control of blacks by means of legal apartheid and the lynch mob, along with "titularly race-neutral vagrancy laws, tenant farming rules, criminal statues, and voter registration and jury selection systems administered to maintain white supremacy."[22] Neither the state officials who wrote the Jim Crow laws nor the local sheriffs and judges whose enforcement powers rested importantly on mob violence worried about either federal interference, or the retribution of black voters. It would be half a century before another protest movement of African Americans would emerge to resume the struggle for emancipation.

Or consider the erosion of the gains made by the twentieth-century labor movement. The strikes and sit-downs that raced through the economy during the the mid-1930s produced heady victories. The Department of Labor reported in 1937 that the wages of rubber workers had increased by one-third over 1934; workers in steel won an industry-wide minimum of five dollars a day, and the industry's wage bill increased by one-third over 1929. Auto workers won a seventy-five-cent-an-hour minimum and a forty-hour workweek. Philip Murray estimated overall that a billion dollars had been added to wages, in steel, automobiles, textiles, transport, and electrical appliances. And when a new dive in the economy in 1937 threatened these gains, Roosevelt called the Congress back from recess for a special session in January 1938 to pass the Fair Labor Standards Act that established a minimum wage affecting some 300,000 workers, and a maximum hours rule that affected an estimated 1,300,000 workers.[23]

Moreover, insurgent workers won the right to collective bargaining. Under the duress of escalating work stoppages, the big companies, including General Motors, U.S. Steel, and Westinghouse, were ready to sign union contracts. "It made sense," says Irving Bernstein, "to negotiate with responsible union officials like John L. Lewis, rather than with desperate local groups."[24] But it was the National Labor Relations Act (NLRA) of 1935 that really built the unions. In April 1937, the Supreme Court handed down its decision in *National Labor Relations Board v. Jones and Laughlin Steel Company* upholding the act and its enforcement mechanism, the National Labor Relations Board (NLRB).

The NLRB required employers to bargain collectively with the elected representatives of a majority of workers; it provided a government mechanism for conducting those elections; and, at the outset, at least, it effectively eliminated the use of such employer weapons as yellow dog contracts, labor spies, and even antiunion propaganda. By the end of 1937, the Congress of Industrial Organizations (CIO) claimed thirty-two affiliated unions, including the giant mass production unions in steel, autos, coal, and rubber. Membership had grown from less than a million in December 1936 to 3.7 million. The American Federation of Labor (AFL) also grew in tandem, and so did the union apparatus of regional offices and state and city central councils.[25] During World War II, strikes were suppressed, but as a result of the War Labor Board's "maintenance of membership" policies, union membership continued to grow, reaching a peak of 35 percent of the labor force by 1945.[26] And improvements in wages continued apace. Between 1936 and the historic 116-day steel strike of 1959, "the average *real* wage of steelworkers increased 110 percent" reports Jack Metzgar, and the average real wage of all manufacturing workers increased by 89 percent.[27]

Metzgar argues strongly and eloquently that unionism was emancipating for industrial workers, a point recently echoed by Andrew Stern, president of the Service Employees International Union:

When we think about auto, steel and rubber workers, before the 1930s and 40s they didn't have high skilled, high wage jobs. But they got a union, and a union job turned out to be a good job, where you could raise a family and enter the middle class.[28]

But it was more complicated than that. Union recognition was a victory, to be sure, but the victory came at a price.

The huge gains of the early decades of the new labor regime were the result of the mobilization of labor's disruptive power, of the strikes and sit-downs during the tumultuous years of the Depression, and of the continuing ability of the unions to reassert that strike power. The new regime of unionism supervised by the National Labor Relations Board was a response to disruption, and was also intended to curb disruption. Spontaneous work stoppages were plaguing the auto industry when GM signed a contract with the United Auto Workers (UAW) that specified there would be no stoppages until an elaborate grievance procedure had been followed and UAW officials had given their approval. The same pattern of spontaneous stoppages led to contracts at Westinghouse and General Electric. The regime was designed to restore normal production by regulating and limiting strike actions, therefore regulating and limiting labor's disruptive power. Union rights were conceded because the unions undertook from the outset to maintain internal discipline in the workplace in exchange for recognition.

Over time, most industrial unions and their members fell in line with the practice of limiting strikes to the termination of contracts.[29] As for the powerful weapon of the sit-down strike, the CIO had never actually endorsed the practice, but with the first big contracts, it quickly disavowed it.[30] By 1950, the United Auto Workers signed a five-year no-strike contract with General Motors, with no protection against the speedup. In 1973, the steelworkers signed an accord with ten major steel companies committing the union not to strike and to submit issues to binding arbitration instead.[31] Taft and Ross sum up the transformation that labor concessions had wrought: "A fundamental purpose of the national labor policy, first enunciated in the Wagner Act and confirmed by its subsequent amendments in the Taft-Hartley and Landrum-Griffin Acts, was the substitution of orderly procedures for trials of combat." And labor law did this "by the establishment of specified rules of conduct imposed on all parties."[32] The unions kept their part of the bargain. Between contracts, they worked to prevent stoppages.

Still, until the 1980s, this "workplace rule of law" created by the National Labor Relations Act was two-sided. Unions forfeited a portion of their disruptive power, since strikes became predictable, and companies could build up inventories to try to outlast the workers. By comparison with the 1930s sit-downs, strikes by and large became tame stuff. Yet, as Jack Metzgar is at pains to emphasize, the rules also protected workers from "arbitrary authority and all the indignities, the humiliation, and the fear that come with being directly subject to the unlimited authority of another human being."[33] Metzgar goes on to describe the steel strikes under this new regime:

> From the first nationwide steel strike in 1946 to the last one in 1959, the Steelworkers would assist the companies in achieving orderly shutdowns, including allowing some workers to cross their own picket line to maintain furnaces that could not be simply turned off. In return, the companies would not even think about trying to breach the line by operating with scabs.[34]

Not, at least, for a while. Management attacks on the workplace rules and wages of the NLRA regime began in the 1950s.[35] By the 1970s, business was on the war path against unions, in the workplace and in electoral politics. It was in fact in the realm of electoral politics that the class battle was joined, and it was in electoral politics that the New Deal labor regime was defeated.

Striking workers had won government protection of the right to organize because the disruption of production was also a threat to the reigning Democratic Party.[36] The electoral fissures that the strike waves threatened forced FDR and the Democrats to push through the big legislative concessions of the mid-1930s. Even as the strike wave peaked, however, union leaders worked hard to develop a more conventional alliance with the Democrats, offering their organizational apparatus, their membership, and their treasuries, presumably in exchange for the political support of the party and its elected officials. In 1936, the CIO unions launched their own campaign to reelect the president, creating a far-flung organization, staging rallies, passing out leaflets, going on radio, and spending nearly a million dollars, while the constituent unions of the CIO contributed another $770,000.[37]

This was only the beginning of the union investment in Democratic Party politics, which in short order took the form of a developed and well-financed campaign organization, capable of canvassing entire communities, in which loyalty to the Democrats was the key. The dream was that the Democratic Party would become a labor party, and indeed, in retrospect, some commentators wax nostalgic and imagine that it was a labor party. But the Democratic Party was also the party of the conservative white South, with its reliance on low-wage labor, and even in the North, big-city bosses continued to wield great influence. The party was pulled in multiple directions, and, perhaps most important of all, a decentralized party was also easily penetrated by business interests. In time, events would show how little the unions would win from electoral politics in return for their loyalty and support.

As the strike threat was tamed, or even before it was tamed, business efforts to roll back government support of the new labor regime began. To be sure, businessmen were not of one mind in this effort. The leading-edge actors were the National Association of Manufacturers (NAM), the Advertising Council, and their allies on the Republican right.[38] As early as 1938, the House Un-American Activities was holding hearings on Communist domination of the CIO, and NAM financed the printing of two million copies of a pamphlet depicting John L. Lewis holding a picket sign high that read, "Join the CIO and Built a Soviet America."[39] Still, although the big industrial corporations were not in the lead, they did not resist these initiatives, which were bearing fruit. In the late 1930s, the Supreme Court ruled that the NLRB could not act to deter unfair labor practices in advance,[40] and by the mid-1940s the composition of the labor board was shifting to include more members sympathetic to employers.[41]

The end of World War II brought an outbreak of strikes led by unions now released from their wartime no-strike pledge, and goaded by the fact that wages had lagged badly against profits during the war. The electoral context that made disruptive strikes so influential in the 1930s had changed, however. Between April 1945 and November 1946, Harry Truman's approval ratings dropped from 87 to 32 percent. And in the midterm elections of November 1946, the Republicans gained eleven seats in the Senate and fifty-six in the House, taking control of Congress for the first time since 1928.

The new Congress responded to the strike threat with the Taft-Hartley Act. The rhetoric with which this and other antilabor initiatives were pushed, says Metzgar, "dripped with antiunion venom."[42] The act began the process of rolling back the National Labor Relations Act. It specified the rights of employers in industrial disputes and restricted the rights of unions; established elaborate reporting requirements regarding internal union procedures; required the officers of unions that wanted the protections of labor law to sign noncommunist affidavits; prohibited various forms of secondary boycotts; outlawed the closed shop; and explicitly allowed the "right to work" laws that were spreading, especially in southern states. This last would turn out to be calamitous for the unions as the mass-production industries began their postwar migration to the Sun Belt. By the late 1950s, as strikes continued, the unions were being tarred in Congress and on television by corruption and racketeering charges, leading to the Landrum-Griffin Act of 1959.

The unions were tamed by these developments, says Jack Metzgar, but they were not defeated. And average real wages continued to increase until 1972.[43] The *Wall Street Journal* recently captured what this meant for many workers, in a story datelined from Milwaukee:

> In 1957, Wayne Hall, then 24 years old, responded to a help-wanted shingle outside Badger Die Casting on this city's south side. He started work the next day, and, over the years, rose from machinery operator to machinery inspector to chief inspector. He helped organize a union, got regular raises, enjoyed generous pension and health benefits and, eventually, five weeks of vacation. At age 72, he is retired and can afford to travel with his wife to Disneyland and Tahiti.[44]

But the numbers of unionized workers had peaked, and in the 1950s, union density began a gradual long-term decline. When the employer assault escalated in the 1970s, even the absolute number of union members plummeted rapidly. The administrative decisions of the NLRB played an important role in the decline, partly as a result of the practice of allowing the backlog of unfair labor practices cases to increase, and partly as a result of rulings that failed to curb employer abuses in union representation election cases.

Of course, changes in the economy were also at work, which gradually weakened the unions based in the mass-production industries. It is these shifts in the postwar American economy that are usually emphasized in accounts of the decline of the New Deal Democratic order. Suburbanization, and the prosperity yielded by unionism itself, loosened the allegiance of manufacturing workers to the Democrats. The migration of industry to the nonunion Sun Belt weakened unions. And globalization eventually led to the shrinkage of the mass production industries. All this happened and shifted the ground on which a labor-based political party could be built.[45] But none of it happened without the cooperation of the Democrats, who promoted the highway subsidies, the water and sewer grants, and the defense industries that spurred suburban and Sun Belt development. Nor did the Democrats mount the big political effort necessary to reverse the provisions of the Taft-Hartley Act that made Sun Belt organizing so difficult. Moreover, the shrinking numbers of manufacturing workers were balanced by expanding numbers of low-wage service sector workers whose Democratic preferences were strong, but for the most part they were not unionized, and neither were they mobilized by the Democratic Party.[46]

It would be a mistake to consider worker victories or setbacks in the struggle for unionization in isolation from broader domestic policies that affect working people, especially policies that supplement incomes and regulate the workplace. The strike movement played a role in winning these policies, and the policies in turn had a large impact on labor markets and working conditions. In fact, the sharp distinctions we often draw between the poor and the working class, or the unemployed, the employed, and the aged, are overdrawn. This is not to deny the persisting animosities between the unemployed—or the irregularly employed—and those with more stable employment. There are multiple reasons for these tensions, ranging from the status anxieties of stable workers, to gender and racial prejudices, to resentments encouraged by the regressive tax systems that pay for income support for the poor, to the opportunistic propaganda of employers and politicians.

Nevertheless, those who were poor and unemployed at one moment became workers at another and also became aged, or were in families with the aged. Even the protest movements were intertwined, in the sense that the militants of the unemployed movement in the 1930s carried their militancy into the workplaces and into the strike movement, as ghetto militants sometimes carried their militancy into union struggles in the 1960s. Moreover, the mobilized unemployed joined with striking workers at crucial moments, as when in the spring of 1934 A. J. Muste's Unemployed League recruited unemployed workers to reinforce the picket lines of the striking auto-parts workers in the "Battle of Toledo."

The concessions won by the movements were also intertwined. In the 1930s the protests by the poor and the unemployed won a comparatively generous if temporary relief system, followed by a public jobs program, also temporary, and then the more long-lasting series of programs authorized by the Social Security Act, including old age and disability pensions, unemployment insurance, and the categorical aid programs we now call "welfare." These programs were obviously important to the poor and the unemployed. They were also important to working people. Labor-market instabilities and the biological exigencies of illness, injury, or old age often forced workers to turn to public benefits. The availability of unemployment insurance, old age assistance, welfare, or Social Security pensions also meant that some people were removed from the competition for work, thus tightening labor markets. Moreover, the very existence of public benefits tended to create a floor beneath which wages could not sink.

In other words, the 1930s movements forced the initiation of at least a minimal American welfare state. The programs were limited and distorted to be sure. Program eligibility and benefits tended to reflect labor-market conditions; those at the bottom of the labor market were also those who were less likely to be protected by the programs. Agricultural and domestic workers, for example, were largely exempted from the protections of the Social Security Act, except for whatever benefits they would be granted from the state-administered categorical assistance programs.

Even limited and conditional programs, however, contributed to the ongoing transformation that the New Deal was effecting in American political culture. The large role that the national government had tried to play in coping with the Great Depression, and especially its initiatives in extending assistance to the poor and working class, changed the way people thought about government, and changed the basis therefore of their political allegiance. In the New Deal Order,[47] voter support increasingly depended less on the tribalist and clientelist appeals that had mobilized participation in the nineteenth century, and more on assessments of whether the regime was contributing to popular economic well-being. This was no small achievement.

Still, after the protest movements of the unemployed, of striking workers, and of the aged subsided in the 1930s, there were no large strides made in the development of the American welfare state comparable to the initiatives of the Depression years. The aged who depended on Social Security benefits remained poor. Harry Truman's efforts to create a national health insurance system went nowhere. The welfare program created in the mid-1930s was administered by the states to largely exclude the black Americans who were being forced off the land in the rural south. It required a new period of protest in the 1960s, spearheaded by African Americans animated by the civil rights movement, to force a considerable liberalization of these programs and prompt the creation of new programs that provided nutritional supplements, health care, and subsidized housing for the poor. But before that happened, the black insurgency achieved another large victory: the restoration of the main planks of Reconstruction-era racial reforms.

The black freedom movement that emerged in the 1950s had complex roots in the new political resources that blacks gained as they moved from the southern agricultural economy to the cities of the South and the North, and in the impact of that transformation on the New Deal Democratic electoral coalition. The forced removal of blacks from the feudal plantation system caused enormous hardship, but it was also a kind of liberation from the near-total social control exerted by the planter, the lynch mob, and the sheriff. Moreover, the subsequent concentration of blacks in the ghettoes of the cities, along with their movement into wage labor, afforded them the protection of sheer concentrated numbers, and in some cases, the political resources of unionization.

Once in the cities, particularly in the northern cities, they also gained the franchise. This turned out to be important because when civil rights protests arose in the south, black voters in northern cities helped to determine Democratic responses.

The New Deal majority coalition was not, of course, simply a coalition of the poor and working class groups who had responded to the progressive initiatives of the 1930s. Rather, those groups had joined a Democratic Party that still included the white South. The New Deal Order was actually a hybrid, formed in part out of the convulsions of the Great Depression, but also including the southern state parties whose allegiance to the Democrats reflected the sectional conflict that led to the Civil War, as well as the realignment of 1896 that had divided the nation into two one-party sections. This peculiar coalition ensured Democratic victories, and it also tempered New Deal initiatives. Southerners in Congress blocked antilynching and fair-employment legislation, made sure that only limited protections would be afforded low-wage workers by New Deal social welfare programs, and ensured that the states would have a large role in administering those programs that might reach the low-wage workforce of the South.

The political repercussions of the economic transformation that pushed growing numbers of African Americans off the plantations and into the cities strained those arrangements. Civil rights demonstrations infuriated the white South but attracted support from northern Democratic constituencies, especially newly enfranchised African American migrants to the cities. Ultimately, the Democrats were forced to concede the Civil Rights Act of 1964, which outlawed discrimination in public accommodations, prohibited federal funding of educational institutions that discriminated, and forbade racial and gender discrimination in employment. A year later the Voting Rights Act of 1965 finally effectively enfranchised southern blacks. These measures spelled the end of the solid white Democratic South, but they also wedded African Americans to the party.

That was not all. The civil rights protests that had begun in the South spread to the northern cities, where conflict was erupting between the growing ghettoes and established white neighborhoods. In an effort to soothe the growing fissures in their northern wing, the

Democratic Party pushed through new initiatives known as the Great Society. The programs initiated in the 1930s were liberalized, and new programs were created that provided food, health care, educational grants, and subsidized housing for the poor.

These initiatives tightened the bonds of African Americans to the Democrats. But the rise of black protest in the northern cities, followed as it was by an upsurge of student protest against the Vietnam War, and then protests by feminists and gays, contributed to the erosion of Democratic support among the white working class, an erosion that had in fact been underway for some time.[48] In 1964, George Wallace, a stalwart of the southern racial order, not only made inroads on the Democratic vote in the South, but also won over 25 percent of the vote in the Democratic primaries in Wisconsin, Indiana, and Maryland. Wallace campaigned also in 1968, when he again made inroads on the Democratic vote, contributing to the Democratic debacle in that election, a falloff from 61 percent of the vote in 1964 to less than 43 percent in 1968.[49]

The costs to the Democrats notwithstanding, the gains resulting from these twentieth-century periods of disruption and reform were substantial. Income and wealth concentration plummeted by half between 1930 and the 1970s.[50] Racial discrimination certainly did not disappear, and African Americans lagged sharply behind whites economically. Black unemployment rates remained twice that of whites, they were much more likely to be poor, and their net worth was a small fraction of their white counterparts.[51] But, however precariously, a good number of blacks were making their way into the middle class, and they had also become voters and acknowledged participants in American political and cultural life.[52]

The dominant political culture also continued to change in the directions ushered in by the New Deal. Political scientists began to take for granted that election results could be predicted from indicators like unemployment rates, or Social Security benefit levels, or changes in personal income.[53] The phenomenon was called, somewhat disparagingly, "pocketbook politics." But pocketbook politics, if it meant the pocketbooks of all the people, was a step toward a more democratic society.

Once the movements subsided, however, the conservative counterassault began to take form. On November 8, 1954, Dwight Eisenhower
had written to his brother John Edgar:

> Should any political party attempt to abolish social security, unem-
> ployment insurance, and eliminate labor laws and farm programs,
> you would not hear of that party again in our political history.
> Among them are H. L. Hunt (you possibly know his background), a
> few other Texas oil millionaires, and an occasional politician or busi-
> ness man from other areas. Their number is negligible and they are
> stupid.[54]

As Eisenhower indicated, business opposition to the New Deal
Order was muted. Memories of the tumult of the 1930s, when business
leaders had lost standing and legitimacy in politics probably played a
role in this,[55] and so did the extraordinary prosperity that American
business enjoyed in the aftermath of World War II. After all, the United
States was the only major industrial power to emerge from the war relatively unscathed. But this golden age of unchallenged American economic domination lasted a mere twenty-five years.

As Europe and Japan recovered, American corporations faced the
unfamiliar prospect of tight competition with goods manufactured elsewhere, and this at a time when they were carrying the costs of the
higher wages, more generous social programs, and workplace and environmental regulations which the turbulent 1960s had produced. By the
early 1970s, as profit margins narrowed, the sorts of business leaders
that Eisenhower had disparaged as marginal and stupid were leading a
conservative counterassault that, as it gained momentum, threatened
to wipe out the reforms of both the New Deal and the Great Society.

The campaign to roll back the New Deal/Great Society reforms
gained momentum as the protest movements of the sixties ebbed.
There were at least four prongs. The first is commonly referred to as
the "war of ideas," with the implication that the laissez-faire arguments
that were revived and expanded in the 1970s were in some significant
sense new. They were not.[56] What was new, rather, was the deliberate
and strategic creation of an apparatus to promulgate these ideas. Rob

Stein, formerly a Democratic political operative, calls it the "message machine."[57] Beginning in the early 1970s, with a handful of small right-wing foundations in the lead, a propaganda apparatus took shape. New think tanks were funded and a handful of older conservative think tanks were enlarged, including the Heritage Foundation, the American Enterprise Institute, the Cato Institute, and the Hoover Institution.

The think tanks elaborated the rollback agenda, making specific proposals for shifting the brunt of taxation from capital to wages, from business and the affluent to working people; to cut back social programs so as to drive more people into the labor force and the scramble for work, and also to keep them anxious and vulnerable about their jobs and their wages; to reduce worker power by weakening unions; to dismantle the environmental and workplace regulations that so irritated business and also cost them money; to reform tort law so as to limit liability suits against corporations; to introduce school vouchers to weaken public schools and especially to weaken the Democratic-leaning teachers union; to build up the military and the defense industry; to toughen law enforcement and build more prisons; and to privatize Social Security.[58]

The new think tanks hired the intellectuals who made the arguments, and spread those arguments widely, on talk shows, in op-ed columns, and so on. Grants from less politically aggressive corporations followed quickly, and the think tanks grew. The lead foundations also launched new periodicals and academic societies and funded right-wing outposts in the universities, particularly in law and economics. They sponsored books by right-wing intellectuals and paid generously to publicize them, including *Freedom to Choose* by Milton Friedman, *Losing Ground* by Charles Murray, and *The Tragedy of Compassion* by Marvin Olasky.

Meanwhile, the right was also developing a formidable media presence with the introduction of the Fox News Channel, *The Rush Limbaugh Show*, Radio America, and the takeover of the editorial board of the *Wall Street Journal*. These outposts in turn spearheaded a campaign to bring mainstream networks, the press, and working journalists into line with a campaign of intimidation. Journalists became terrified of being labeled "liberal," or, more recently, of being charged with a lack of patriotic ardor.[59] Just as important, media companies were gobbling each other up, and these vastly larger media corporations were natural allies in the business campaign.[60] The Corporation for Public Broadcasting was a special target. Republicans persistently attempted to cut its funding, and by 2005 had succeeded in appointing a former cochair of the Republican National Committee as its next president and chief executive.[61]

The second prong was the buildup of the lobbying capacity of business, with the creation of new peak organizations, the revival of sleepy old organizations like the Chamber of Commerce and the National Association of Manufacturers, the invention of business-backed "Astroturf" strategies that lent the business agenda a populist cast, and the buildup of a war machine in Washington, D.C., known as K Street. These groups did not merely pressure government from the outside; they invaded government, as key lobbyists were promoted to government posts, and others sat with congressional committees to draft legislation.[62]

The third prong was the cultivation of the populist right, rooted in fundamentalist churches. The growth of these right-wing groups was in a way fortuitous and distinguished this period from earlier eras of business domination. The rise of a pro-life movement, the defense-of-marriage groups, the Christian Right, the rifle groups, and so on—all of this was no doubt owed more to the anxieties provoked by changes in American society that are often associated with the cultural currents of the 1960s, including racial liberalism and changing sexual and family mores. But whatever their roots, it was the genius or good fortune of the strategists of the business right to manage to bring the populist right into the fold.

This odd alliance was sealed with propaganda that, in Linda Kintz's words, "spiritualized the market economy"[63] by joining market fundamentalism to Christian fundamentalism. Corporate entrepreneurs "more than any other class of men . . . embody and fulfill the sweet and mysterious consolations of the Sermon on the Mount," pontificated George Gilder.[64] Market fundamentalism is of course simply old-fashioned laissez-faire, a doctrine in which the individual stands naked and unprotected before market forces and market "law." Christian fundamentalism also strips the individual of communal and political supports, although now the individual stands naked and unprotected before God, and God's law. As Mike Gecan, an Industrial Areas Foundation community organizer, writes:

> The religious resonance is reinforced by an economic resonance that is also deep and powerful. The president's "ownership society" is based on a vision of an individual who is capable of having a direct and personal relationship with the market. An individual should have control over his or her own economic destiny—should be able to own a home rather than renting, work for a private business rather than for the government, save money for retirement rather than expecting the government or an employer to make the arrangements. . . . The president is asserting that the individual person or family doesn't need mediating institutions and programs. . . . [T]hese institutions and programs have disrupted the development of the hoped-for relationship between the person and the market, just as many believers feel that denomination and religious bureaucracies impede the growth of the personal relationship with God.[65]

God and the market are abstractions, however, and the campaign did not rely on abstractions. The organized right had a better symbol at hand. The propaganda of the message machine emphasized welfare, welfare recipients, and the Great Society, all codes to evoke and mobilize popular anxieties, and to turn the populist right against the programs and the political culture of the New Deal/Great Society period.

There were good reasons for this strategy. The people on welfare were already marginalized and vulnerable. Paupers have always been a despised caste in Western societies. Add to this longstanding distaste the fact that, in the wake of the mass migration of African Americans from the rural South to the urban North and the protests that ensued in the 1960s, welfare had become a disproportionately black (and Hispanic) program. The presidential campaigns of Barry Goldwater and George Wallace registered this fact and made evident the political uses to which it could be put. "Welfare" became a code word to evoke and mobilize rising white racial hatreds.

At the same time, changing sexual and family mores were stirring a backlash of popular anxieties, anxieties that were fueled even more by the rise of the feminist movement. Since most recipients were single mothers, and black or brown, they were easily made into the symbol that captured all of this agitated hate politics. Ronald Reagan made the image of the "welfare queen" a staple of American popular culture. This was the politics of spectacle, a spectacle designed to evoke and intensify popular antipathies against Democrats, against blacks, against liberals, against licentious women, and against government, or at least those parts of government that provided support to poor and working people. In the background and out of the spotlight was the longer term campaign of the organized right to defeat and dismantle the New Deal/Great Society political order.

The fourth prong was the successful effort to change the major political parties. Together, the alliance of business and the populist right took over the Republican Party, pouring new money into the electoral campaigns of hard-right candidates and pushing older-style conservatives to the margins. Business and business money was important in this process. Note, for example, that in 1980 big business broke with its usual practice of contributing to both major parties. The funds flowed to the Reagan campaign, and Reagan won. Then again in the midterm election of 1994, business money tilted overwhelmingly to the Republican congressional races, and the Republicans swept Congress, winning the House for the first time in many years, elevating Newt Gingrich to the speakership, and making the Contract with America and its distinguishing slogan of personal responsibility a template for its legislative initiatives.

But the real measure of the political success of the campaign was its influence on the Democratic Party, which had, for all its internal conflicts, and however reluctantly, championed the New Deal/Great Society order. Franklin Delano Roosevelt had talked of "strong central government as a haven of refuge to the individual."[66] By the 1990s, this tenet of the New Deal/Great Society was jettisoned by the Democrats, and welfare politics played a key role. The decades-long campaign that turned welfare into a metaphor for African Americans, sexual license, and liberalism had done its political work. In 1992, Bill Clinton made his bid for the presidency on the slogan of "ending welfare as we know it." As the 1996 election approached, the Republicans held his feet to the fire with their proposal for rolling back welfare, called the Personal Responsibility and Work Opportunity Reconciliation Act. He turned for advice to his pollsters and consultants. Dick Morris told him to "fast-forward the Gingrich agenda." "Progressives," argued Clinton pollster Stanley B. Greenberg, "needed to transcend welfare politics."[67] Clinton signed the measure. The Democratic strategy, in a nutshell, was to beat the Republicans by adopting their positions.[68]

All of the loud talk notwithstanding, welfare was a small program. The agenda of the campaign was much larger and is by now familiar: shift the brunt of taxation from business and the affluent to working people, and from capital to wages; roll back income support programs so as to increase insecurity among workers or potential workers.

Federal taxation has been rolled back massively, especially the taxation of private capital. Obviously, these measures make the rich richer. The scale of the cuts also ensures continuing pressure to cut social programs. As deficits grow, the specter of fiscal crisis eviscerates the capacity, or at least the will, of the federal government to fund social welfare or regulatory programs.[69] "Proposing to slash federal spending, particularly on social programs, is a tricky electoral proposition, but a fiscal crisis offers the tantalizing prospect of forcing such cuts through the back door," says the Financial Times, adding "The lunatics are now in charge of the asylum."[70] "Market theology and unelected leadership," says Kevin Phillips, "have been displacing politics and elections."[71]

"So what has shifted the balance" of power between workers and employers, asks the Financial Times. And the Times goes on to name among other causes the fact that companies feel there is an abundance of workers to draw on.[72] The abundance of workers, in turn, is a reflection of new government policies. Social benefit cuts obviously drive more people to seek work, often as part-timers or temps. Federal income support and service programs have been scaled back, most famously by the radical retrenchment of the 1930s welfare program for mothers and children, but also through less-noticed cutbacks in unemployment insurance, housing, and nutritional and childcare programs. And there are more cuts in the offing. Medicaid, the federal health insurance program for low-income people, and the State Children's Health Insurance Program which reaches low income children, are slated for especially big cuts, and in any case, the state governments that administer the programs are already dropping hundreds of thousands of people from the rolls.[73] Even the Earned Income Security Credit program, which gives modest subsidies to twenty-one million low-wage workers and was once applauded by both parties for supporting work, not welfare,[74] is in the sights of the budget cutters, as are housing and community development programs.[75]

Immigration policies that leave the borders relatively open but bar immigrants from social welfare protections also contribute to an abundance of workers, even though the administration that presides over these policies simultaneously indulges the vigilante Minutemen who have now undertaken to patrol the Mexican border. So, too, does the assault on pensions enlarge the numbers looking for work. As the private plans won by unionized workers from their employers after World War II were shifted from defined-benefit pensions to lower-cost 401(k)s, employers saved money, but pension benefits shrank.[76] At the same time, employer-controlled pension funds became the target of plunder by management. As retirement benefits plummet, inevitably more of the old will continue to work.[77]

Falling wages also drive more people into the labor market for more hours, and weaker unions are part of the reason for falling wages. Beginning in the 1970s, big employers began to scuttle the union agreements that had marked the period of the labor accord, not only resisting new union demands at contract negotiations, but demanding givebacks, and successfully resisting the recognition of new unions. President Ronald Reagan made his mark by firing striking air controllers in his first year in office. The policy assault against unions continued in the efforts to eviscerate legal protections for labor, including minimum-wage protections (which were allowed to fall steadily behind inflation), overtime pay requirements, pensions, workplace safety regulation, and the right to unionize, the last mainly as a result of the failure of the National Labor Relations Board to effectively protect labor rights.

George W. Bush regularly used his presidential powers to weaken unions. He issued executive orders that ended labor-management partnerships in the federal government, barred project-wide collective bargaining agreements on federally funded public works projects, required federal contractors to post notices advising workers of their right *not* to join a union, imposed a sixty-day ban on job actions by machinists at United Airlines, and directed the Department of Justice to seek a Taft-Hartley injunction to end the shutdown of West Coast docks. Workplace safety rights have been dismantled, the budget of the Occupational Safety and Health Administration has been slashed, federal jobs have been put up to bid by private contractors, employees in the Department of Homeland Security and airport screeners have been stripped of collective bargaining rights, and so on. The unions, already decimated by the contraction of the mass production industries, are reeling, their density levels down to levels before the New Deal.

Over time, as the campaign gained momentum and scored successes, the agenda became more ambitious and greedier. Not only were the social programs to be slashed, but what remained of them was targeted as another arena for profitability through publicly subsidized privatization. Families squeezed between stagnant wages and rising costs resorted increasingly to borrowing, and some were driven into bankruptcy. Then, in an effort spearheaded by the banks and credit card companies, even the protections to ordinary families offered by bankruptcy law were rolled back.

Ordinary Americans have already lost a great deal.

Social Security is the largest income support program, it has always been intensely popular, and it is the hallmark of the New Deal. This has not protected it from rollbacks, and the Bush administration has targeted the program in a scheme for gradual privatization that threatens future benefits. In this instance, Democrats rallied to defend the program, and at this writing, there is a standoff on the issue. But this particular campaign has been long in the making, a definitive defeat will not be easy, and there is no reason to be confident that the program will survive in its current form.

Environmental regulations are steadily being eroded, with the familiar justification that voluntary and market-based solutions are more effective. This is a problem that affects not just the United States but, given the scale of the American economy and its production of pollutants, the entire planet. An international consortium of scientists recently warned of potentially irreversible and catastrophic increases in global warming that would melt most of the polar ice caps, raise sea levels by more than twenty feet, and leave London under water. [78]

These policy setbacks go far toward explaining what is perhaps the most notable feature of the contemporary period, the striking rise in wealth and income inequality over the past quarter of a century as the income and wealth share of the poorer and middle strata shrink, the top 1 percent grows much richer, and the very richest grows vastly richer.[79] Concentrated wealth and the power it yields to affect decisions is itself in large measure a consequence of government tax, regulatory, social, and monetary policies that favor holders of wealth. And as wealth concentration grows, so does the arrogance and the power that it yields to the wealth-holders to continue to bend government policies in their own interest.

Finally, there is the turn by the U.S. government to unilateral military aggression abroad and the dangers it entails, for other peoples as well as Americans. Multilateral arrangements are weakened, terrorism flourishes, and the U.S. regime flounders in incompetence. Moreover, jingoism and the war fever it nourishes have provided the political cover for many of the aggressive new assaults on domestic policy, as taxes on the affluent are repeatedly slashed, military spending grows, and domestic social programs continue to be whittled away, or turned into spoils for private contractors.

This, broadly, is the dimension of our problem. The forces arrayed against democratic influence are formidable, the scale of change required even to redress the losses of the past few decades is large, and compounding the problem are deep flaws in the electoral-representative arrangements to which we usually look for democratic redress of the abuses of power. American politics has once again fallen under the domination of business, its historic default position in the absence of popular insurgency.

Epilogue

ILL THE NEAR-TOTAL domination by business and its right-wing allies of national politics be reversed by another period of popular upheaval? This is the big question for our time, a question important for Americans and, because the United States exerts such powerful influence on the fate of other peoples, increasingly across the planet.

The answer cannot be certain, and is surely not simple. The classical view is that hardship itself propels people to collective defiance, especially in the context of growing concentrations of income and wealth. But much of our historical experience reveals that people endure hardship more often than they protest it, and even extreme inequality does not necessarily lead people to see their circumstances as unjust.

The righteous indignation that propels movements is nourished when people see ways of acting on their felt problems. Injustice is not even injustice when it is perceived as inevitable. The cultural strategies of the right are designed to encourage Americans to accept contemporary U.S. policies by imbuing them with the aura of inevitability. The right-wing message machine revives the doctrine of laissez-faire, the idea that free markets are the way of nature or the way of God, and that the policies of the right are molded by this spiritualized market law. These are of course the nineteenth-century beliefs that were overridden during the New Deal/Great Society era when the idea that government could and should be responsible for our collective well-being gained ascendance. But laissez-faire beliefs were not eradicated, and they are being revived. Moreover, the belief in markets as natural law and God's law gains a certain awesome power in our time as a result of the internationalization of market exchanges. Laissez-faire doctrine was always a doctrine of inevitability, of fatalism, at least for those at the bottom end of economic exchanges. In an era when the movement of goods, capital, and labor across borders seems to escape the control of the nation-state, laissez-faire ideas gain weight. And as they do, they threaten to stamp out the conviction that has made democracy so compelling through the centuries, the idea that if people control the state, they can influence their collective destiny.

Moreover, in at least some ways the policies of the right reinforce the political ideas that fuel right-wing politics. The concentration of income and wealth among the most affluent augments their political resources and strengthens their righteous self-confidence in their own advantages and the policies that produce those advantages.[1] Meanwhile, the growing misery of the poor, and especially of the very poor, may stimulate contempt among the larger public more than sympathy and thus deepen their marginality. The seediness and inadequacy that results from stripping the public sector of funds encourages distaste with public services and facilities, especially when the affluent increasingly turn to private services and gated communities. The ownership society initiatives—the shift from guaranteed pensions to stock accounts, the rollback of subsidized housing in favor of shaky schemes for home ownership, and the proposals for "medical savings accounts"—encourage delusions about the prospect of somehow striking it rich in the market. Hardship and insecurity lead more and more people to turn to religion, especially to right-leaning evangelical and often fundamentalist churches that offer not only eternal salvation, but the concrete assistance that government programs no longer provide, including child care, after-school programs, support groups of various kinds, and even cash handouts. The Bush administration encourages this trend with its faith-based initiatives which channel government funds to help churches provide the services that government once provided, creating a new system of clientelism, especially in the African American and Hispanic communities which have until now been bastions of the Democratic Party. Meanwhile, appeals to family values may resonate just because family life is hollowed out when parents are stressed by overwork. "Over the last 30 years, workers in middle-income, married-couple families with children have added an average of 20 more weeks at work, the equivalent of five more months."[2] Long hours at work by both parents mean that no one has the time to do the caring tasks—the meal preparation, the homework help, the holidays, the play dates, and the family outings—that are the stuff of family life.

And then there are the distortions of political judgment that result from the "war on terror" which the regime has exploited to increase its political support. As everyone knows, George W. Bush assumed the presidency in the 2000 election as a result of a Supreme Court decision. Not only was the election disputed, but the economy was moving into recession and Bush was falling in the polls. Then the planes hit the towers in New York City, and Bush was able to recast himself as the anointed leader of a nation at war. The excitement and fear that can be stirred up when leaders point to foreign threats that people inevitably cannot assess on the basis of their own experience is a form of mystification. It is a mystification that has served the right-wing campaign well.

So, this is indeed a troubled moment in American political life. But popular political ideas are more complicated and more fluid than this catalogue of right-wing propaganda successes suggests. One way that they are more complicated is that most people believe more than one thing at a time. They may respond to exhortations for personal responsibility and still harbor the faith in collective responsibility nourished by the New Deal/Great Society, which in fact is what the survey data do indeed suggest. Then, also, the patriotic fervor generated by war tends to fade over time as the costs of war to the population become evident, and sometimes also as the deceits that accompanied war making are exposed. By mid-2005, only 37 percent of the public approved of the administration's handling of the war in Iraq, and a mere 25 percent agreed with the president's proposals on Social Security.[3]

There is another complication that I think is more important and that also points in a more hopeful direction. There is, I believe, an intimate connection between what people think is possible in politics and what they think is right. These two sorts of judgments continually influence one another. People do not complain about the inevitable, and certainly they do not mobilize to change what they think is inevitable, but once new possibilities for change that are within the reach of ordinary people become evident, or at least once people think they are evident and within reach, popular aspirations also expand. This is why the doctrine of inevitability associated with a spiritualized market economy operating at a global scale can be so pernicious. And it is also why we should think not only about the "oughts" of a new political agenda, but about the potential for popular power under contemporary conditions.

In the aftermath of the deeply flawed 2000 and 2004 elections, when charges of corrupt procedures in the handling of voter registration, balloting, and vote counting abounded, a good many commentators made lists of the electoral reforms that were needed. The proposals were all reasonable. We should have a national right to vote, a universal system of voter registration, consistent ballot design, and national rules on voter identification requirements and on the counting and recounting of ballots. Election day should be a national holiday, election administration should be nonpartisan, computer voting technology should be transparent and provide a secure paper trail, and so on. These reforms would indeed remedy some of the flaws in our electoral procedures, and everything I have said until now argues that elections are important, especially in mediating the impact of protest movements. The threat posed by disruptive movements of fractionalizing majority voter coalitions would be more potent if the electorate were more inclusive and if elections were fairer. But a more inclusive electorate and fairer elections would also affect the reelection chances of incumbent politicians and their parties. Short of a tremendous electoral upset, the reforms that would broaden voter turnout and guarantee a more accurate vote count are not likely to be implemented by the incumbent politicians who benefit from the way American elections are now conducted.

What, then, are the prospects for the emergence of new social movements that mobilize disruptive power? Colin Crouch says in reference to those who criticized the antiglobalization demonstrators in Seattle, London, and Prague for their violence and their anarchism, "We must ask ourselves: without a massive escalation of truly disruptive actions . . . will anything reverse the profit calculations of global capital enough to brings its representatives to the bargaining table? That is the question which most challenges the health of contemporary democracy."[4] In fact, the demonstrations in Seattle, London, and Prague hardly tapped the possibilities for disruptive power in the twenty-first century.

Much of the current discussion of this question has focused on organized labor, where a big debate is raging about strategies to reverse the decline in membership. Most of the discussion is about the internal organization of labor. One strand of criticism is of the dominant "service" model that directs most union resources toward the needs of existing members instead of toward organizing the unorganized. Others call for a more democratic and movement-oriented unionism. "We need," say Bob Master and Hetty Rosenstein, "to engender a militant, organizing culture in our unions . . . with a model that emphasizes rank-and-file education and action."[5] Or more simply, labor needs to become a social movement again. And as I write, the AFL-CIO confronts a challenge from dissident unions led by Service Employees International who have pulled out of the federation, presumably because their proposals were not adopted. They wanted to spend most of the unions' treasuries on organizing, and they also wanted to consolidate the federation's fifty-eight affiliates so that there would be only one union for each industry, a restructuring which they argue would curb intraunion competition and increase the organizing capability of the consolidated unions by increasing their membership and treasuries.[6]

These may be reasonable proposals. But I am skeptical about the almost total preoccupation with the organizing problem instead of the power problem. The assumption is that if the unions did the right thing in their own house, then union membership would grow, and the power of labor would increase. It may be that the causality should be reversed. After all, even now a majority of American workers say they would join a union if they could. But employers have made it increasingly difficult even to try, by mounting campaigns that threaten and frighten workers when a union campaign is in the offing, by blocking access by union organizers to the work site, and by outright violations of such legal protections as remain, especially by illegally firing workers who choose the union.[7] Bill Pastreich, a veteran labor organizer now organizing Wal-Mart workers, reports that the "associates" who are purportedly so loyal to the company "are about the same as other workers—same issues, same percent unhappy and willing to do something—just no good strategy to help them."[8]

Perhaps if the unions could demonstrate that mobilized workers can face down recalcitrant employers, then workers would brave those risks and flock to the unions. The big rush to join unions in 1933 was mainly a response to the excitement and promise generated by the election of a president who promised to look to the forgotten man, and the passage of legislation that announced (though it did not in fact provide for implementation) "the right to organize and bargain collectively."[9] The president's words, and the words of the National Industrial Recovery Act, were understood to spell out the promise of power. Similarly, union density in the public sector was declining in the late 1950s. "But then a critical mass of organizing, politics, and highly visible strikes came together in the early 1960s, setting off a stampede of public sector unionism beginning in 1962."[10] Maybe workers need to see the possibility of worker power again.

In other words, labor activists, whether union organizers or not, need to concentrate on developing and demonstrating power strategies that are effective in the "new economy," increasingly a service economy, a high-tech economy, and a global economy. The conventional wisdom is that these developments have all sapped worker power. They have indeed sapped a particular expression of worker power, the power that was achieved when industrial workers shut down the rubber plants, auto plants, or steel plants, for example. Now there are far fewer such plants, and far fewer such workers. Even in those manufacturing plants that still exist, the old power of the strike seems not much power at all when companies can shift production elsewhere. No wonder strike rates have plummeted, along with inflation-adjusted wages and union membership as well.[11]

But the new economy has its own distinctive vulnerabilities. To be sure, the reliance on outsourcing and offshoring that characterizes the global production system seems at first glance simply to weaken workers because it gives employers the flexibility to exit in the face of worker demands. However, the reliance on outsourcing and offshoring, and the extended chains of production and distribution that are inevitably entailed, also creates multiple junctures of interdependence. These systems are complex and fragile, and their operation depends on the cooperation of far-flung networks of workers, consumers, and sometimes even people who are neither workers nor consumers. The simultaneous reliance on "just-in-time production" exacerbates the fragility of these systems. Manufacturers once built up inventories to weather the strikes that were threatened when contracts expired. With strikes less likely, the cost-saving system of just-in-time production has taken hold. But just-in-time inventories, along with lean production methods, make manufacturers more vulnerable, not less, to work and distribution stoppages, were they to occur.

Edna Bonacich and Jake B. Wilson illustrate this point in their discussion of the potential for organizing Wal-Mart's "logistics" workers, by which they mean workers responsible for transportation and distribution. Like all Wal-Mart workers, these workers are being hard pressed by the cost-cutting pressures of the Wal-Mart system. They propose a campaign against the company that seeks out its production and distribution vulnerabilities and stretches across its global logistical chains.

> Wal-Mart depends on [just-in-time] production and distribution of goods. . . . In addition, the fact that global production depends on extended supply lines means that these lines can be cut by organized strikes and protests. Globally produced goods must pass through critical chokepoints, such as ports and nearby transportation and warehousing systems, which would be especially vulnerable to such actions. Global logistics can be seen as the Achilles' heel of global production.[12]

The ability of dockworkers and truck drivers to "shut it down" is of course legendary, and it applies to global systems as well as national systems of production. But it is not just the old logistics workers that have forms of power in the new economy that are so far largely untapped. The sweatshop campaign that mobilized American consumer power in defense of worker rights in low-wage countries suggested the possibility of reconstruction on a global scale of the worker-consumer alliances that were important in American labor struggles in the early twentieth century. Those alliances were made possible by local community ties. The Internet creates the possibility of constructing similar ties of sympathy that do not depend on local proximity.

The Internet is significant for another reason. It adds another dimension to the fragility and vulnerability of contemporary institutions. Hackers have demonstrated this, even though their disruptions seem so far to be largely mischievous in intent, albeit not entirely without political meaning. After all, while the world's attention was focused on the demonstrations in the streets of Seattle in November 1999, thousands of "hactivists" worked to shut down the World Trade Organization servers. And across the Southern Hemisphere, people are emerging from the presumed backwaters of traditional economies to occupy land and facilities and block roads in order to influence national and even international policies. These are only hints of the forms that disruptive power challenges might take in the future.

New conditions will require new forms of political action, new "repertoires" that both extend across borders and tap the chokepoints of new systems of production and new systems of governance, the points at which they are vulnerable to the collective defiance of ordinary people. They may also require new leaders less tied to inherited repertoires and the organizations that rely on them. My point in this book is not to lay out a blueprint for the future, but to show that all of our past experience argues that the mobilization of collective defiance and the disruption it causes have always been essential to the preservation of democracy.

Notes

Chapter One

1. Robert Dahl sums up the minimal requirements for a democratic country as (1) elected officials; (2) free, fair and frequent elections; (3) freedom of expression; (4) alternative sources of information; (5) associational autonomy; and (6) inclusive citizenship. See "What Political Institutions Does Large-Scale Democracy Require?" *Political Science Quarterly* (Summer 2005): 188.

2. Stephen Ansolabehere and his colleagues have calculated the distortions in state funding to counties that resulted from the population disparities in state legislative districts before court-ordered redistricting in the 1960s. See Stephen Ansolabehere, Alan Gerber, and James Snyder, "Equal Votes, Equal Money: Court-ordered Redistricting and Public Expenditure in the American States," *American Political Science Review* 96, no.4 (December 2002): 779–77.

3. Richard P. McCormick, "The Party Period and Public Policy: An Exploratory Hypothesis," *Journal of American History* 66, no. 2 (September 1979).

4. Kevin Philips, *Wealth and Democracy: A Political History of the American Rich* (New York: Broadway Books, 2002), 414.

5. Joseph Schumpeter, *Capitalism, Socialism, and Democracy* (New York: Harper, 1947), 269.

6. E. E. Schattschneider, *Party Government* (New York: Rinehart, 1942), 15.

7. Powell reports that Western democracies with proportional representation systems that encourage third parties were more responsive to dissidents. In effect, third parties substitute for protest movements. See G. Bingham Powell, *Contemporary Democracies* (Cambridge, MA: Harvard University Press, 1982).

8. See Elizabeth Drew's description of what she describes as "the unprecedented corruption—the intensified buying and selling of influence over legislation and federal policy—that has become endemic in Washington," in "Selling Washington," *New York Review*, June 23, 2005, 24–27.

9. On this point, see Colin Crouch, *Coping with Post-Democracy* (Glasgow: Bell & Bain, 2000), 35.

10. On the GOP business political machine, see Nicholas Confessore, "Welcome to the Machine: How the GOP disciplined K Street and made Bush Supreme," *Washington Monthly Online*, July/August 2003.

11. See "Tomgram: Mark Danner on Smoking Signposts to Nowhere," www.tomdispatch.com/index.mhtml?pid=3602. Frank Rich reports that in the 19 press briefings by the White House after the "Downing Street memo" was revealed, only 2 out of 940 questions by the press corps were about the memo. See "Don't Follow the Money," *New York Times*, June 12, 2005. There are numerous similar examples of the suppression of news unfavorable to the reigning administration by the mainstream media. Todd Gitlin gives the example of the failure of the media to report the number of detainees who died in American custody during the "war on terror." See "MIA: News of Prison Toll," *The Nation*, July 4, 2005.

12. For one journalist's list of right-wing media outlets, see Lewis Lapham, "Tentacles of Rage: The Republican propaganda mill, a brief history," *Harper's*, September 2004.

13. Editorial, "Squelching Public Broadcasting," *New York Times*, June 15, 2005.

14. Bill Moyers, "A Moral Transaction," TomPaine.com, June 20, 2005.

15. David Cay Johnston, "Tax Laws Help to Widen Gap at Very Top," *New York Times*, June 5, 2005, 1.

16. These numbers are from a study by Citizens for Tax Justice, reported in David E. Rosenbaum, "Bush May Have Exaggerated, but Did He Lie?" *New York Times*, Week in Review section, June 22, 2003, 1. For an excellent analysis of the distortions of voter perceptions with regard to the new tax legislation, see Jacob S. Hacker and Paul Pierson, "Abandoning the Middle: The Bush Tax Cuts and the Limits of Democratic Control," *Perspectives on Politics* 3, no. 1 (March 2005): 33–53.

17. Robert Pear, "Inquiry Sought for Charge of Threat Over Medicare Data," *New York Times*, March 14, 2004; Robin Toner, "Seems the Last Word on Medicare Wasn't," *New York Times*, March 17, 2004; Robert Pear, "Medicare Official Testifies on Cost Figures," *New York Times*, March 25, 2004. See also Elizabeth Drew, "Hung Up in Washington," *New York Review*, February 12, 2004; and Frances Fox Piven, *The War at Home: The Domestic Costs of Bush's Militarism* (New York: New Press, 2004), 83–85.

18. Eventually Tom DeLay, the author of the redistricting plan, came under fire in the House for a series of ethics violations involving his ties to lobbyists and the travel jaunts he accepted from them. The chairman of the House ethics committee investigating the charges turned out to have a close relationship with the Seattle-based law firm at the center of the ethics accusations against DeLay. See Philip Shenon, "House Ethics Chief Is Tied to Lobby Figures," *New York Times*,

June 8, 2005. By the fall of 2005, Delay was under indictment in Travis County, Texas, for conspiracy and money laundering in connection with these maneuvers.

19. In the fall of 2005, auditors from the Government Accountability Office sharply criticized this practice as illegal and "covert propaganda." See Robert Pear, "Buying of News by Bush's Aides Is Ruled Illegal," *New York Times*, October 1, 2005.

20. Fred Block, "The Right's Moral Trouble," *The Nation*, September 30, 2003.

21. Colin Crouch, *Coping with Post-Democracy (Fabian Ideas)* (Glasgow: Bell & Bain, Ltd, 2000), 2.

22. See Kevin Phillips, *Arrogant Capital: Washington, Wall Street, and the Frustration of American Politics* (Boston: Little, Brown and Company, 1994), 8; Dan Balz and Ronald Brownstein, *Storming the Gates: Protest Politics and the Republican Revival* (Boston: Little Brown and Company, 1996), 12–13.

23. Steven J. Rosenstone and John Mark Hansen, *Mobilization, Participation, and Democracy in America* (New York: Macmillan, 1993), 216.

24. Cited in Phillips, *Arrogant Capital*, 8.

25. Robert Putnam, *Bowling Alone: The Collapse and Renewal of American Community* (New York: Simon and Schuster, 2000), 41.

26. Rosenstone and Hansen, *Mobilization, Participation, and Democracy in America*, 226.

27. For a discussion, see Frances Fox Piven and Richard A. Cloward, *Why Americans Still Don't Vote* (Boston: Beacon Press, 2000), chap. 12.

28. Robert Dahl and Charles Lindblom, *Politics, Economics, and Welfare* (New York: Harper and Row, 1953).

29. Dahl and Lindblom, *Politics, Economics, and Welfare*, xxxi

30. Robert A. Dahl, *How Democratic Is the American Constitution?* (New Haven, CT: Yale University Press, 2001), 115.

31. The United States now ranks highest among rich countries in each of seven measures of inequality. Moreover, a front-page leader in the *Wall Street Journal* concluded, "Despite the widespread belief that the U.S. remains a more mobile society than Europe, economists and sociologists say that in recent decades the typical child starting out in poverty in continental Europe (or in Canada) has a better chance at prosperity." *Wall Street Journal*, May 13, 2005:1. For a summary of the data on inequality and some of its political implications, see the American Political Science Association Task Force on Inequality and American Democracy, "American Democracy in an Age of Rising Inequality," *Perspectives on Politics* 2, no. 4 (December 2004): 651–75.

32. See Sidney Verba, Kay Lehman Schlozman, and Henry E. Brady, *Voice and Equality: Civic Voluntarism in American Politics* (Cambridge, MA: Harvard University Press, 1995).

33. For a discussion of these preoccupations in early American political thought, see Michael J. Thompson, "The Politics of Inequality: A Political History of Economic Inequality in America." (PhD dissertation, Political Science Program, Graduate Center of the City University of New York, 2005).

34. A number of contemporary analysts suggest that economic oligarchy undermines democratic ideology. See Paul Krugman, "For Richer," *New York Times Magazine*, October 20, 2002; Frank Levy, *The New Dollars and Dreams: American Incomes and Economic Change* (New York: Russell Sage Foundation, 1998); and the review article by Alexander Hicks pointing to data presented by these and other sources on the correlation between income concentration at the top and Republican conservatism, "Back to the future? A review essay on income concentration and conservatism," *Socio-Economic Review*, no. 1 (2003): 271–88.

35. For a discussion, see Thomas Ferguson, "Holy Owned Subsidiary: Globalization, Religion, and Politics in the 2004 Election," in William Crotty, ed., *A Defining Election: The Presidential Race of 2004* (Armonk, NY: M. E. Sharpe, 2005).

36. Sheldon Wolin, "Political Theory as a Vocation," *American Political Science Review* 63 (1969): 1062–1082.

37. Joshua Cohen and Joel Rogers, *On Democracy: Toward a Transformation of American Society* (New York: Penguin Books, 1983).

38. Phillips, *Arrogant Capital*, 29.

39. Paul Krugman, "Standard Operating Procedure," *New York Times*, June 3, 2003, A31.

40. See, for example, the descriptions in Alexis de Tocqueville, *Democracy in America* (New York: Anchor Books, 1969), 242–43; Samuel P. Hays, "Politics and Society: Beyond the Political Party," in Paul Kleppner, ed., *The Evolution of American Electoral Systems* (Westport, CT: Greenwood Press); and William E. Gienapp, "'Politics Seem to Enter into Everything': Political Culture in the North, 1840–1860," in Stephen E. Maizlish and John Kushman, eds., *Essays on Antebellum Politics, 1840–1860* (College Station: Texas A&M University Press, 1982).

41. Quoted by Mark Green, "Stamping Out Corruption," *New York Times*, October 28, 1986, A35, and cited in Bertell Ollman and Jonathan Birnbaum, eds. *The United States Constitution* (New York: New York University Press, 1990), 7–8.

42. Kevin Phillips, *Wealth and Democracy*, 201.

43. See "The Omaha Platform of the People's Party of America (July 4, 1892),'" in Howard Zinn and Anthony Arnove, *Voices of a People's History of the United States* (New York: Seven Story Press, 2004), 229.

44. See Elizabeth Sanders, *Roots of Reform: Farmers, Workers and the American State, 1877–1917* (Chicago: University of Chicago Press, 1999), 94.

45. Louise Overacker, *Money in Elections* (New York: Macmillan, 1932). Cited in Jeff Manza et al., "Money, Participation, and Votes: Social Cleavages and Electoral Politics," in *Handbook of Political Sociology*, ed. Thomas Janoski et al. (Cambridge: Cambridge University Press, 2004).

46. Michael Tomasky, "Texas-Sized Problem," *The American Prospect*, May 2005: 19.

Chapter Two

This chapter is drawn from Frances Fox Piven and Richard A. Cloward, "Rulemaking, Rulebreaking, and Power," in *Handbook of Political Sociology*, ed. Thomas Janoski et al. (Cambridge: Cambridge University Press, 2005).

1. See Randall Collins, *Conflict Sociology: Toward an Explanatory Social Science* (New York: Academic Press, 1975), 60–61.

2. See C. Wright Mills, *The Power Elite* (New York: Oxford University Press, 1956), 9, 23. This point about the organizational of power was later developed by Robert Presthus, *Men at the Top: A Study in Community Power* (New York: Oxford University Press, 1964).

3. See Charles Tilly, *Mobilization to Revolution* (Reading, MA: Addison-Wesley Publishing Co. 1978), 69.

4. Georg Wilhelm Friedrich Hegel, "The Phenomenology of the Spirit," in *The Philosophy of Hegel*, ed. Carl J. Friedrich (New York: Random House, 1953), 399–411.

5. I am not making a case for the centrality of disruption for the first time. That the distinctive power of protest movements is rooted in disruption has indeed been the signature argument in much of my long collaboration with Richard Cloward. See Frances Fox Piven, "Low Income People and the Political Process, in *The Politics of Turmoil: Essays on Poverty, Race and the Urban Crisis*, ed. Frances Fox Piven and Richard A. Cloward (New York: Pantheon Books, 1974); Frances Fox Piven and Richard A. Cloward, *Poor People's Movements: Why They Succeed, How They Fail* (New York: Pantheon Books, 1979); and Richard A. Cloward and Frances Fox Piven, "Disruptive Dissensus: People and Power in the Industrial Age," in *Reflections on Community Organization*, ed. Jack Rothman (Ithaca, IL: F. E. Peacock, 1999).

6. Alberto Melucci, "Ten Hypotheses in the Analysis of New Movements," in *Contemporary Italian Sociology*, ed. Diana Pinto (Cambridge: Cambridge University Press, 1981), 173–94.

7. Ronald Aminzade, "Between Movement and Party: The Transformation of Mid-Nineteenth Century French Republicanism," in *The Politics of Social Protest:*

Comparaative Perspectives on States and Social Movements, ed. J. Craig Jenkins and Bert Klandersmans (Minneapolis: University of Minnesota Press, 1995), 40.

8. See Richard M. Emerson, "Power-Dependence Relations," *American Sociological Review* 27 (February 1962): 31–40, and Peter Blau, *Exchange and Power in Social Life* (New York: John Wiley and Sons, 1964), 118.

9. For a discussion of societies as overlapping, intersecting power networks that generate "promiscuous" sources of power, see Michael Mann, *The Sources of Social Power,* vol. 1 (New York: Cambridge University Press, 1986), chap. 1.

10. See Norbert Elias, *Power and Civility* (New York: Pantheon Books, 1982).

11. See Joseph Schumpeter, "The Crisis of the Tax State," in *International Economic Papers,* no. 4 (New York: Macmillan Co., 1954), 5–38.

12. See Michael Lipsky, *Protest in City Politics: Rent Strikes, Housing and the Power of the Poor* (Chicago: Rand McNally, 1970). See also Michael Lipsky, "Protest as a Political Resource," *American Political Science Review* 62 (1968): 1046-56.

13. See Ray Raphael, *A People's History of the American Revolution* (New York: New Press, 2001), 19.

14. See Charles Tilly, Louise Tilly, and Richard Tilly, *The Rebellious Century, 1830-1930* (Cambridge, MA: Harvard University Press, 1975), 288.

15. See Charles Tilly, *The Politics of Collective Violence* (New York: Cambridge University Press, 2003).

16. See James Weinstein, *The Long Detour: The History and Future of the American Left* (Boulder, CO: Westview Press, 2003), 51–52.

17. See Lance Hill, *The Deacons for Defense: Armed Resistance and the Civil Rights Movement* (Chapel Hill: University of North Carolina Press, 2004).

18. See Gay Seidman, "Guerrillas in Their Midst: Armed Struggle in the South African Anti-Apartheid Movement," *Mobilization* 6, no. 2 (2001): 11–127.

19. See Naomi Klein, "Baghdad Year-Zero," www.truthout.org/docs_04/092604E.shtml.

20. "Instead of bothering about abstract and timeless definitions and determinations . . . we need to describe and explain . . . precisely those complex and characteristic conjunctions of work, everyday life, appropriation, accumulation, and hegemony that class informs." Kalb considers that "class analysis then becomes a narrative strategy, focusing on the historically-embedded, shifting relationships between social groups as they are linked through production and reproduction, alternating between micro and macro levels, and accounting for the complex social processes in which they become entwined, which structure their chances and resources, and which are perpetually kept going by their actions and interactions." See Don Kalb, *Expanding Class* (Durham, NC: Duke University Press, 1997), Introduction.

21. William Sewell, "A Theory of Structure: Duality, Agency and Transformation," *American Journal of Sociology* 98 (July 1992).

22. George Simmel makes the point that the ruler himself becomes subject to the law he promulgates. See *The Sociology of George Simmel*, ed. Kurt H. Wolff (Glencoe, IL: The Free Press, 1950), 263.

23. See Barrington Moore, *The Social Origins of Dictatorship and Democracy* (Boston: Beacon Press, 1965), 470–74.

24. E. P. Thompson, *The Making of the English Working Class* (New York: Vintage, 1963), chap. 14.

25. This is a point that Richard Cloward and I have made before. "[R]iots require little more by way of organization than numbers, propinquity, and some communication. Most patterns of human settlement . . . supply these structural requirements." See Frances Fox Piven and Richard Cloward, "Normalizing Collective Protest" in *Frontiers in Social Movement Theory*, ed. Aldon D. Morris and Carol Mueller (New Haven, CT: Yale University Press, 1992), 310.

26. Stathis N. Kalyvas's discussion of civil wars provides a useful analogy. Civil wars, says Kalynas, "are not binary conflicts but complex and ambiguous processes that foster an apparently massive, though variable, mix of identities and actions." See "The Ontology of 'Political Violence': Action and Identity in Civil Wars," *Perspectives on Politics* 1, no. 3 (September 2003): 475.

27. See Raymond J. Walsh, *CIO: Industrial Unionism in Action* (New York: W. W. Norton and Co., 1937), 49.

28. Walsh, *CIO*, 171.

29. See the following chapters by Charles Tilly: "The Web of Contention in Eighteenth-Century Cities," in *Class Conflict and Collective Action*, ed. Louise A. Tilly and Charles Tilly (Beverly Hills, CA: Sage, 1981), 27–51; "Social Movements and National Politics," in *Statemaking and Social Movements*, ed. Charles Bright and Susan Harding (Ann Arbor: University of Michigan Press, 1984), 308; "Britain Creates the Social Movement," in *Social Conflict and Political Order in Modern Britain*, ed. James E. Cronin and Jonathan Schneer (New Brunswick, NJ: Rutgers University Press, 1982), 21–51.

30. There are many accounts of these events. See in particular Nick Salvatore, *Eugene V. Debs: Citizen and Socialist* (Urbana: University of Illinois Press, 1982). See also Weinstein, *The Long Detour*.

31. Tilly, "Social Movements and National Politics," 308. For an effort to solve theoretical problem of the relationship of structure to agency in the development of repertoires, see Ruud Koopmans, "The Missing Link Between Structure and Agency: Outline of an Evolutionary Approach to Social Movements," *Mobilization* 10, no. 1 (February 2005): 19–35.

32. On this point, see Piven and Cloward, "Normalizing Collective Protest," 301–25.

Chapter Three

1. See James A. Morone, *The Democratic Wish: Popular Participation and the Limits of American Government* (New York: Basic Books, 1990), 54.

2. This point is now widely agreed. The pivotal work was probably Carl L. Becker, *The History of Political Parties in the Province of New York* (Madison: University of Wisconsin Press, 1909). See also Alfred Young's influential collection, *The American Revolution: Explorations in the History of American Radicalism* (DeKalb: Northern Illinois University Press, 1976); Carl Bridenbaugh, *Cities in Revolt: Urban Life in America, 1743-1776* (New York: Knopf, 1955); Bernard Bailyn, *Pamphlets of the American Revolution, 1750-1776* (Cambridge, MA: Harvard University Press, 1965); Edmund S. Morgan, *The Birth of the New Republic, 1763-1789* (Chicago: University of Chicago Press, 1956); Arthur Schlesinger, "Political Mob in the American Revolution," *Proceedings of the American Philosophical Society* 99 (1955).

3. "While any social relationship is by definition organized in some sense or other, to organize it *politically* is to construct and enforce explicit or implicit rules for making and implementing decisions about how the relationship is to be lived," Austin Turk, *Political Criminality: The Defiance and Defense of Authority* (Beverly Hills, CA: Sage Publications, 1982), 14.

4. On the sometimes precarious dependencies of the tax state, see Joseph A. Schumpeter, "The Crisis of the Tax State," *International Economic Papers*, no. 4 (New York: Macmillan Co., 1954), 5–38.

5. Markoff makes this point. See John Markoff, *Waves of Democracy: Social Movements and Political Change* (Thousand Oaks, CA: Pine Forge Press, 1996), 41.

6. Translated and quoted by Jack A. Goldstone and Bert Useem, "Prison Riots as Microrevolutions: An Extension of State-Centered Theories of Revolution." *American Journal of Sociology* 104, no. 4 (January 1999): 989.

7. The pages that follow are adapted from an earlier essay coauthored with Richard A. Cloward, "Eras of Protest, Compact, and Exit: On How Elites Make the World and Common People Sometimes Humanize It," in *State Theory Reconsidered: Paradigm Lost*, ed. Stanley Aronowitz and Peter Bratsis (Minneapolis: University of Minnesota Press, 2002), 143–69.

8. Political challenge by the lower strata often does not take obvious and explicit forms, for the simple reason that open challenge risks severe reprisals. On this point, see John Markoff, *Waves of Democracy: Social Movements and Political*

Change (Thousand Oaks, CA: Pine Forge Press, 1996). See also James C. Scott, *Weapons of the Weak* (New Haven, CT: Yale University Press, 1985).

9. See Catherine Lis and Hugo Soly, *Poverty and Capitalism in Pre-Industrial Europe* (Atlantic Highlands, NJ: Humanities Press, 1979), 115. See also Robert Jutte, *Poverty and Deviance in Early Modern Europe* (New York: Cambridge University Press, 1993), and Christopher Hill, "Puritans and the Poor," *Past and Present* 2 (November 1952): 32–50.

10. For a more extended discussion, see Richard A. Cloward and Frances Fox Piven, "Eras of Protest, Compact, and Exit: On How Elites Make the World and Common People Sometimes Humanize It," in *State Theory Reconsidered: Paradigm Lost*, ed. Stanley Aronowitz and Peter Bratsis (Minneapolis: University of Minnesota Press, 2002).

11. Karl Polanyi, *The Great Transformation* (Boston: Beacon Press, 1957), 92.

12. George Rudé, *The Crowd in History* (New York: John Wiley and Sons, 1964).

13. Charles Tilly, "Food Supply and Public Order in Modern Europe," in *The Formation of Nation States in Western Europe*, ed. Charles Tilly (Princeton, NJ: Princeton University Press, 1975).

14. E. P. Thompson, "The Moral Economy of the English Crowd in the Eighteenth Century," *Past and Present* 50 (February 1971), 76–136.

15. Thompson, "The Moral Economy," 115.

16. See Miles Taylor, "Six Points: Chartism and the Reform of Parliament," in *The Chartist Legacy*, ed. Owen Ashton, Robert Fyson, and Stephen Roberts (Woodbridge, England: Merlin,1999), 1–23.

17. Dorothy Thompson, *The Chartists: Popular Politics in the Industrial Revolution* (New York: Pantheon Books, 1984), Preface.

18. Rogers M. Smith has been at pains to point out the starkly inegalitarian conditions and ideas that also prevailed in the colonies, including chattel slavery, patriarchy, and the conquest of indigenous people and their lands. See Rogers M. Smith, *Civic Ideals* (New Haven, CT: Yale University Press, 1997). See also by Smith, "Substance and Methods in APD Research," *Studies in American Political Development* 17 (Spring 2003): 111–15.

19. See Charles Tilly, "Introduction," in *Class Conflict and Collective Action*, ed. Louise A. Tilly and Charles Tilly (Beverly Hills, CA: Sage Publications, 1981), 20. Tilly also makes this point about the similarity of the crowd's repertoire on both sides of the Atlantic. See "The Web of Contention," in Tilly and Tilly, *Class Conflict*, 27–48.

20. See Keith I. Polakoff, *Political Parties in American History* (New York: Alfred A. Knopf, 1981), 4.

21. See James A. Morone, *The Democratic Wish*, 37. The actual suffrage requirements varied from colony to colony. Almost all the colonies made property a

requirement for suffrage, but property ownership was more widespread than in England. Bernard Bailyn attributes an explosive democratic potential to colonial electoral arrangements. See *The Ideological Origins of the American Revolution* (Cambridge, MA: Harvard University Press), 1967.

22. "The independence of the New Worlds from the Old Order," writes Goran Therborn, "may legitimately be called a part of a 'democratic revolution.' " "The Right to Vote and the Four World Routes to/through Modernity," in *State Theory and State History*, ed. Rolf Torstendahl (Beverly Hills, CA: Sage Publications, 1992), 74.

23. See Pauline Maier, *From Resistance to Revolution: Colonial Radicals and the Development of American Opposition to Britain, 1765-1776* (New York: Alfred A. Knopf, 1972), 3.

24. Edward Countryman, *The American Revolution* (New York: Hill and Wang, 2003), 30.

25. Howard Zinn, *A People's History of the United States* (New York: Harper and Row, 1980), chaps. 3 and 4.

26. See Ray Raphael, *A People's History of the American Revolution* (New York: New Press, 2001), 11–12.

27. For an exhaustive review of the extraordinary surge of popular defiance against authority during the decades surrounding the revolution, see Gary B. Nash, *The Unknown American Revolution: The Unruly Birth of Democracy and the Struggle to Create America* (New York: Viking, 2005).

28. On rural protests, see Raphael, *People's History of the American Revolution*, 25–31; Countryman, *The American Revolution*, 68–69, 73–80; Zinn, *People's History of the United States*, 62–64.

29. Paul A. Gilje, *Rising in America* (Bloomington: Indiana University Press, 1996), 44–45, cited in Raphael, *People's History of the American Revolution*, 27–28.

30. Schlesinger, "Political Mob in the American Revolution," 244.

31. Morone, *The Democratic Wish*, 47.

32. See Carl Becker, *The History of Political Parties in the Province of New York, 1760-1776* (Madison: University of Wisconsin Press, 1968).

33. New York Public Library, *Bancroft Transcripts, America, 1765-1766*, 151, cited in Chilton Williamson, *American Suffrage: From Property to Democracy 1760-1860* (Princeton, NJ: Princeton University Press, 1960), 78; *Bancroft Transcripts, 1766-1767*, 268, cited in Williamson, *American Suffrate*, 78; See Morone, *The Democratic Wish*, chap. 1; Countryman, *The American Revolution*, chap. 2. See also O. M. Dickerson, *The Navigation Acts and the American Revolution* (Philadelphia: University of Pennsylvania Press, 1951).

34. Williamson, *American Suffrage*, 78

35. Countryman, *The American Revolution*, 80–81.

36. Countryman, *The American Revolution*, 36.

37. There is a substantial historical record documenting the interplay of war-making and democratic initiatives. See, for example, Geoff Eley, *Forging Democracy: The History of the Left in Europe, 1850-2000* (Oxford: Oxford University Press, 2002), chap. 7; Goran Therborn, "The Rule of Capital and the Rise of Democracy," *New Left Review* 103 (1977); Dietrich Rueschemeyer, Evelyn Huber Stephens, and John D. Stephens, *Capitalist Development and Democracy* (Chicago: University of Chicago Press, 1992); Charles Tilly, *Coercion, Capital, and European States, AD 990-1990* (Cambridge, MA: Basil Blackwell, 1990).

38. Williamson, *American Suffrage*, 88

39. Williamson, *American Suffrage*, 82–83.

40. Williamson, *American Suffrage*, 103.

41. Gordon Woods, *The Creation of the American Republic, 1776-1787* (New York: W. W. Norton, 1969), 18.

42. See Peter Linebaugh for an interesting argument that traces popular democratic aspirations, and their linkage with the struggle for subsistence rights, as far back as the Magna Carta. The provisions that registered these aspirations are, he says, the ones we don't remember. "The Secret History of the Magna Carta," *Boston Review* (Summer 2003).

43. Margaret Somers traces democratic convictions to the participatory arrangements that existed in local government in rural England in the 1700s. See Margaret Somers, "Citizenship and the place of the public sphere: Law, Community and political culture in the transition to democracy," *American Sociological Review* 58, no. 5: 587–620.

44. Quoted in Wood, *The Creation of the American Republic*, 18.

45. See John A. Guidry and Mark O. Sawyer, "Contentious Pluralism: The Public Sphere and Democracy," *Perspectives on Politics* 1, no. 2 (June 2003), 274.

46. Alexander Keyssar, *The Right to Vote: The Contested History of Democracy in the United States* (New York: Basic Books, 2000), 16.

47. See Polakoff, *Political Parties in American History*, 8–10.

48. Wood, *The Creation of the American Republic*, 404.

49. Gordon Wood recounts the charges of the Vermont Council of Censors: "The legislature . . . was reaching for 'uncontrolled dominion' in the administration of justice: becoming a court of chancery . . ., interfering in causes between parties, reversing court judgments, staying executions . . ., and even prohibiting court actions in matters pertaining to land titles or private contracts." Wood, *The Creation of the American Republic*, 407.

50. Keyssar, *The Right to Vote*, 1.

51. Wood, *The Creation of the American Republic*, chap. 11. Merrill Jensen concludes that the conservatives made only occasional gains in the states, helping them to realize that "centralization was their *protection*." See Merrill Jensen, "The Articles of Confederation," in *The United States Constitution: 200 Years of Anti-Federalist, Muckraking, Progressive and Especially Socialist Criticism*, ed. Bertell Ollman and Jonathan Birnbaum (New York: New York University Press,1990), 19.

52. See Polakoff, *Political Parties in American History*, 13.

53. Wood, *The Creation of the American Republic*, 467.

54. Jackson Turner Main defines the contest between the Federalist nation-builders who promoted the Constitution and their Anti-Federalist opponents as "a contest between the commercial and the non-commercial elements in the population." See Jackson Turner Main, *The Antifederalists: Critics of the Constitution, 1781-1788* (Chapel Hill: University of North Carolina Press: 1962).

55. Wood, *The Creation of the American Republic*, 476.

56. See Michael Parenti, "The Constitution as an Elitist Document," in *The United States Constition*, ed. Ollman and Birnbaum, 146.

57. Federal systems that allow this degree of autonomy and power to subnational governments are relatively rare. See Robert A. Dahl, *How Democratic Is the American Constitution?* (New Haven, CT: Yale University Press, 2001), 42.

58. For an excellent contemporary discussion of the impact of American federalism on class political power, see Jacob S. Hacker and Paul Pierson, "Business Power and Social Policy: Employer and the Formation of the American Welfare State," *Politics and Society* 30, no. 2 (June 2002): 277–325.

59. On the upper chamber as a body representing the ancient regime, see Goran Therborn, "The Right to Vote and the Four World Routes to/through Modernity," 71.

60. Dahl says of the unequal representation that resulted from these several arrangements that they reveal "a profound violation of the democratic idea of political equality among all citizens." See Dahl, *How Democratic Is the American Constitution?* 49

61. Keyssar, *The Right to Vote*, 21.

62. Countryman, *The American Revolution*, 190.

63. The authority of the Supreme Court to override actions by the other branches on constitutional grounds was, however, the result of judicial interpretation, and probably not intended by the founders. See, for example, Ferdinand Lundberg, "Court over Constitution," in *The United States Constitution*, ed. Ollman and Birnbaum, 187–200.

64. Dahl, *How Democratic Is the American Constitution?* 19.

65. Wood, *The Creation of the American Republic*, 610.

66. Jensen, "The Articles of Confederation," 24.

67. Main, *The Antifederaistst*. See also Thomas Ferguson, "Party Realignment and American Industrial Structure," *Research in Political Economy* 6 (1983): 33.

68. On this point, see Dahl, *How Democratic Is the American Constitution?* 3

69. Keyssar, *The Right to Vote*, 25.

70. The white male franchise was delayed for decades, however, in Rhode Island, where it became entangled in the question of the black male franchise. For an exhaustive treatment, see Christopher Malone, "Between Freedom and Bondage: Racial Voting Restrictions in the Antebellum North," Ph.D. Dissertation, the Graduate School and University Center, City University of New York, 2004.

71. Barrington Moore, *Social Origins of Dictatorship and Democracy: Lord and Peasant in the Making of the Modern World* (Boston: Beacon Press, 1966), 112–13.

72. Edmund S. Morgan, "The Other Founders," *New York Review*, September 22, 2005, 43.

73. A century later, a broadly similar crisis of governability led to the expansion of democratic arrangements in Europe. See Geoff Eley, *Forging Democracy: The History of the Left in Europe, 1850-2000* (New York: Oxford University Press, 2002). See also Dennis Pilon, "Why do Voting Systems Change? Electoral Reform in Western Industrialized Countries" (thesis submitted to the Faculty of Graduate Studies in partial fulfillment of the requirements for the degree of Doctorate of Philosphy, Department of Political Science, York University, Toronto, 2005).

Chapter Four

1. Roberta Ash Garner and Mayer Zald, "The Political Economy of Social Movement Sectors," in *Social Movements in an Organizational Society*, ed. Mayer N. Zald and John McCarthy (New Brunswick, NJ: Transactions, 1990), 293–318.

2. See Barrington Moore, *Social Origins of Dictatorship and Democracy: Lord and Peasant in the Making of the Modern World* (Boston: Beacon Press, 1966), 127.

3. E. E. Schattschneider, *Party Government* (New York: Rinehart & Co., 1942), 65.

4. See Colin Crouch, *Coping with Post-Democracy (Fabian Ideas)* (Glasgow: Bell & Bain, 2000), 4.

5. Chilton Williamson, *American Suffrage: From Property to Democracy, 1760–1860* (Princeton, NJ: Princeton University Press, 1960), 76. See also Alexander Keyssar, *The Right to Vote: The Contested History of Democracy in the United States* (New York, Basic Books, 2000), chap. 2.

6. James MacGregor Burns, *The Vineyard of Liberty* (New York: Alfred A. Knopf, 1982), 364.

7. See Dietrich Rueschemeyer, Evelyne Huber Stephens, and John D. Stephens, *Captialist Development and Democracy* (Chicago: University of Chicago Press, 1992), 124; and Thomas Ferguson, "Party Realignment and American Industrial Structure: The Investment Theory of Political Parties in Historical Perspective," in *Research in Political Economy*, v. 6, ed. P. Zarembla (Greenwich, CT: JAI Press, 1983).

8. See John Aldrich, *Why Parties? The Origin and Formation of Party Politics in America*, (Chicago: University of Chicago Press, 1995), 106.

9. Aldrich, *Why Parties?* 106.

10. Giovanni Sartori, *Parties and Party Systems* (Cambridge: Cambridge University Press, 1976), ix.

11. Aldrich, *Why Parties?* 77.

12. The big expansion of the franchise that stimulated this development was mainly in the right to vote for presidential electors. See Aldrich, *Why Parties?* 106. See also Richard P. McCormick, "New Perspectives on Jacksonian Politics, *American Historical Review* 65 (January): 288–301.

13. Burns, *The Vineyards of Liberty*, 421.

14. See Aldrich, *Why Parties?* chap. 4.

15. Charles Dickens to Charles Sumner, March 13, 1842, quoted in Norman and Jeanne MacKenzie, *Dickens: A Life* (Oxford: Oxford University Press, 1979), 120.

16. The number of states using a statewide, winner-take-all procedure for tabulating the votes of the electoral college increased as the franchise expanded. Aldrich reports that in 1824, twelve states used the method, while six used a district method. By 1828, the number of states using the winner-take-all procedure had increased to eighteen, while only four used a district method. See Aldrich, *Why Parties?* 307–308, n. 12.

17. See Deborah Gray White, "Let My People Go, 1804–1860, in *To Make Our World Anew: A History of African Americans*, ed. Robin D. G. Kelly and Earl Lewis (Oxford: Oxford University Press, 2000), 201.

18. The Virginia General Assembly authorized the liberation of slaves who substituted for their owners during the war, but many planters in fact reenslaved veterans, and those who had served in the navy were sold by the Commonwealth. See Art Budros, "Social Shocks and Slave Social Mobility: Manumission in Brunswick County, Virginia, 1782–1862," *American Journal of Sociology* 110, no. 2 (November 2004): 547.

19. See Daniel Littlefield, "Revolutionary Citizens, 1776–1804," in *To Make Our World Anew*, ed. Kelley and Lewis, 117.

20. See Littlefield, "Revolutionary Citizens," 155.

21. Roger L. Ransom, *Conflict and Compromise: The Political Economy of Slavery, Emancipation, and the American Civil War* (Cambridge: Cambridge University Press, 1989), 18.

22. Ransom, *Conflict and Compromise*, 30.

23. Quoted by Staughton Lynd, "The Abolitionist Critique of the United States Constitution," in *The Antislavery Vanguard: New Essays on the Abolitionists*, ed. Martin Duberman (Princeton, NJ: Princeton University Press, 1965), 218.

24. Lynd, "The Abolitionists," 224.

25. Frederick Douglass, "The Constitution and Slavery," *North Star*, March 16, 1849.

26. Garry Wills, "The Negro President," *New York Review of Books* 50, no. 15 (November 26, 2003).

27. Michael Goldfield, *The Color of Politics: Race and the Mainsprings of American Politics* (New York: New Press, 1997), 79.

28. Thomas Jefferson hailed his ascendance to the presidency in 1800 as a triumph of democracy. He won by a margin of eight electoral votes, and at least twelve of his total votes were based on the three-fifths rule. See Gary Wills, "The Negro President."

29. The delegates from South Carolina and Georgia declared they would not join the union if the slave traffic were simply prohibited. See Douglass, "The Constitution and Slavery."

30. The relation of slave to master was understood as a labor contract, for life. See Ransom, *Conflict and Compromise*, 29.

31. See Littlefield, "Revolutionary Citizens, 134.

32. Goldfield, *The Color of Politics*. Table 4.1 takes these numbers from Stuart Weems Bruchey, *Cotton and the Growth of the American Economy, 1790–1860* (New York: Harcourt, Brace, and World, 1967), table 3A. See also Zinn, *A People's History of the United States*, 167; and Herbert Aptheker, *Abolitionism: A Revolutionary Movement* (Boston: Twayne Publishers, 1989), 4, 29.

33. Moore, *Social Organizations of Dictatorship and Democracy*, 116.

34. On the role of New York bankers in the Southern cotton crop, see Richard Rubinson, "Political Transformation in Germany and the United States," in *Social Change in the Capitalist World Economy*, ed. Barbara Hockey Kaplan (Beverly Hills, CA: Sage Publications, 1978), 39–73. Similarly, Ferguson reports that by 1828, when proposals for annexing Texas were being debated, many businessmen from New York, Boston, Philadelphia, and the South were heavily invested there. Ferguson, "Party Realignment and American Industrial Structure," 38.

35. See Robert V. Remini, *Martin Van Buren and the Making of the Democratic Party* (New York: Columbia University Press, 1959), 5–6, cited in Aldrich, *Why Parties?* 108.

36. See James L. Sundquist, *The Dynamics of the Party System: Alignment and Realignment of Political Parties in the United States* (Washington, DC: The Brookings Institution, 1973), 40–41.

37. See Ransom, *Conflict and Compromise*, 92.

38. Marc Egnal, "The Beards Were Right: Parties in the North, 1840–1860," *Civil War History* 47, no. 1 (March 2001): 38.

39. For evidence on this point, see Lynd, "The Abolitionist Crtique."

40. See Ransom, *Conflict and Comrpromise*, 104.

41. Aptheker quotes a letter from a South Carolinian to President James Monroe blaming the debate over Missouri for the Vesey plot: "The discussion of the Missouri question at Washington, among evils, produced this plot." See Herbert Apthetker, *Racism, Imperialism and Peace: Selected Essays* (Minneapolis: MEP Publications, 1987), 81.

42. Aptheker, *Race, Imperialism, and Peace*, 8.

43. Ransom, *Conflict and Compromise*, 39.

44. On the role of the "balance rule" in granting statehood in preserving peace between the sections, see Barry R. Weingast, "Political Stability and Civil War: Institutions, Commitment, and American Democracy," in *Analytic Narratives*, ed. Robert Bates, et al. (Princeton, NJ: Princeton University Press, 1998).

45. See Aldrich, *Why Parties?* 128–33.

46. Keith I. Polakoff, *Political Parties in American History* (New York: Alfred A. Knopf, 1981), 161.

47. Ransom, *Conflict and Compromise*, 96.

48. Cited in Sundquist, *The Dynamics of the Party System*, 57.

49. See John Hope Franklin, *From Slavery to Freedom: A History of Negro Americans* (New York: Vintage, 1969).

50. Sundquist, *Dynamics of the Party System*, 60.

51. Eric Foner, *Free Soil, Free Labor, Free Men* (London: Oxford University Press, 1971), 192.

52. Foner, *Free Soil, Free Labor, Free Men*, 5.

53. Egnal, "The Beards Were Right."

54. Winders, employing a "class segments" analysis, adopts and elaborates this particular explanation. See Bill Winders, "Changing Racial Inequality: The Rise and Fall of Systems of Racial Inequality in the U.S." (paper delivered at the annual meeting of the American Sociological Association, San Francisco, CA, August 2004).

55. See Moore, *Social Origins of Dictatorship and Democracy*, 152.

56. Howard Zinn, "Abolitionists, Freedom-Riders, and the Tactics of Agitation," in *The Antislavery Vanguard: New Essays on the Abolitionists*, ed. Martin Duberman (Princeton, NJ: Princeton University Press, 1965), 417.

57. See Littlefield, "Revolutionary Citizens,"108, on early Quaker antislavery initiatives.

58. David Brion Davis, "The Quaker Ethic and the Antislavery International," in *The Antislavery Debate: Capitalism and Abolitionism as a Problem in Historical Interpretation*, ed. Thomas Bender (Berkeley: University of California Press, 1992).

59. See Littlefield, "Revolutionary Citizens," 133.

60. Littlefield, "Revolutionary Citizens," 168.

61. See Dwight Lowell Dumond, *Antislavery: The Crusade for Freedom in America* (Ann Arbor: University of Michigan Press, 1961), 87–95.

62. Franklin, *From Slavery to Freedom*, 263.

63. Eisenstadt discusses the central role that religion plays in American social movements generally. See S. N. Eisenstadt, *Paradoxes of Democracy: Fragility, Continuity, and Change* (Baltimore, MD: Johns Hopkins University Press, 1999), Chap. 7.

64. Foner, *Free Soil, Free Labor, Free Men*, 109. See also Littlefield, "Revolutionary Citizens," 107–8.

65. See Paul Kleppner, *The Third Electoral System, 1853–1892: Parties, Voters and Political Cultures* (Chapel Hill: University of North Carolina Press, 1979), 59–74; also by Paul Kleppner, "Partisanship and Ethnoreligious Conflict: The Third Electoral System, 1853–1892, in *The Evolution of American Electoral Systems*, ed. Paul Kleppner et al. (Wesport, CT: Greenwood Press, 1981), 113–46.

66. Quoted in Franklin, *From Slavery to Freedom*, 244.

67. Quoted in Zinn, "Abolitionists, Freedom-Riders, and The Tactics of Agitation," 418.

68. Sundquist, *The Dynamics of the Party System*, 44.

69. Franklin, *From Slavery to Freedom*, 246. See also Aptheker, *Abolitionism*, xiii.

70. Polakoff, *Political Parties in American History*, 147–48.

71. See Sundquist, *The Dynamics of the Party System*, 47.

72. See Littlefield, "Revolutionary Citizens," 150–51.

73. See Stanley M. Elkins, *Slavery: A Problem in American Institutional and Intellectual Life* (New York: Grosset & Dunlap, 1963), 184–85. For a detailed account of the role of the abolitionist minister, see also Donald Mathews, "Orange Scott: The Methodist Evangelist as Revolutionary," in *The Antislavery Vanguard*, ed. Duberman, 71–101.

74. Orren and Skowronek at least suggest this possibility: "[C]hanges within religious denominations at this time bore down on the institutions of democracy and slavery alike, both holding the antebellum polity together and breaking it apart." See Karren Orren and Stephen Skowronek, *The Search for American Political Development* (Cambridge: Cambridge University Press, 2004), 17.

75. Franklin, *From Slavery to Freedom*, 248.

76. See Goldfield, *The Color of Politics*, 94.

77. Fawn M. Brodie, "Who Defends the Abolitionist?" in *The Antislavery Vanguard*, ed. Duberman, 58.

78. Sundquist quotes Theodore Clarke Smith: "In the track of every mob abolitionist societies sprang up like mushrooms." See Theodore Clarke Smith, *The Liberty and Free Soil Parties in the Northwest* (New York: Russell and Russell, 1897), 17, cited in Sundquist, *The Dynamics of the Party System*, 44.

79. Polakoff, *Political Parties in American History*, 147–48.

80. Eugene D. Genovese, *Roll, Jordan, Roll: The World the Slaves Made* (New York: Pantheon Books, 1972), 585–658; see also Littlefield, "Revolutionary Citizens," 197.

81. See Franklin, *From Slavery to Freedom*, 205–8; White, *op. cit*, 197.

82. Marilynne Robinson, "Freed: Victims of the African slave trade, captured en masse in Senegal, Sierra Leone &c., for shipping in chains across the sea to lifelong servitude," *New York Times Book Review*, January 9, 2005.

83. See Littlefield, "Revolutionary Citizens," 160–68.

84. Aptheker, *Abolitionism*, 76. The largest slave rebellion in the British West Indies occurred in Jamaica at the end of 1831. It led to the death of hundreds of slaves, but it also was influential in the events that led to the emancipation of slaves in the British Empire, on August 1, 1838. See Adam Hochschild, "Against All Odds," *Mother Jones*, January/February 2004.

85. Franklin, *From Slavery to Freedom*, 210.

86. See Zinn, *People's History*, 169; White, "Let My People Go," 197.

87. The alliance between blacks and the Seminoles was long lasting, and Seminole lands were a refuge for fleeing slaves, helping to account for Andrew Jackson's determination to seize Seminole land. See White, "Let My People Go," 197.

88. See Goldfield, *The Color of Politics*, 78, 80.

89. Zinn, *People's History*, 170.

90. Deborah Gray White writes that nineteenth-century slaveholders tried to improve the imperial conditions of slaves because "deep down" they understood that slavery led to resistance. Perhaps the rebellions of the century helped to drive that lesson home. See White, "Let My People Go," 198.

91. See White, "Let My People Go," 199–210.

92. Aptheker, *Abolitionism*, 67.

93. Franklin, *From Slavery to Freedom*, 253–60.

94. Franklin cites Wilbur H. Siebert for the estimate that the Underground Railroad had 3200 active workers. See Franklin, *From Slavery to Freedom*, 210.

95. Quoted in White, "Let My People Go," 219.

96. Franklin, *From Slavery to Freedom*, 210. See also Fergus M. Bordewich, *Bound for Canaan: The Underground Railroad and the War for the Soul of America* (New York: Amistad, 2005), who estimates some 100,000 slaves were helped to escape over the course of the nineteenth century. Drew Faust offers a skeptical view of the scale and organization often attributed to the railroad, but acknowledges its potent impact on the politics of the period. See "Trainspotting," *The Nation*, May 23, 2005, 46–48.

97. The quote is from W. E. B. Du Bois, *John Brown* (New York: International Publishers, 1962), quoted in Zinn, *People's History*, 181.

98. Sundquist, *The Dynamics of the Party System*; Steven J. Rosenstone, Roy L. Behr, and Edward H. Lazarus, *Third Parties in America: Citizen Response to Major Party Failure* (Princeton, NJ: Princeton University Press, 1984), 49–50.

99. Horace Greeley to R. M. Whipple, April 1860, quoted in Egnal, "The Beards Were Right," 44.

100. Sundquist, *The Dynamics of the Party System*, 42.

101. See Ransom, *Conflict and Compromise*, 102.

102. Rosenstone, Behr, and Lazarus think Democratic splintering was also motivated by patronage disputes. See *Third Parties in America*, 52.

103. For a discussion of fissures in the Democratic Party, see Foner, *Free Soil, Free Labor, Free Men*, 150–55.

104. Michael Holt, however, in his exhaustive study of state-level Whig parties, gives little weight to the antislavery cause in the ensuing events, emphasizing instead party politics. See Michael F. Holt, *The Rise and Fall of the American Whig Party: Jacksonian Politics and the Onset of the Civil War* (New York: Oxford University Press, 1999). See also the critical review of Holt's book by John Ashworth, "The Whigs, the Wood, and the Trees," *Reviews in American History* 28 (2000): 215–22.

105. See Rosenstone, Behr, and Lazarus, *Third Parties in America*, 60. See also Polakoff, *Political Parties in American History*, 153.

106. Kleppner, *The Third Electoral System*, 66.

107. Kleppner reports declining turnout numbers both in the North and the South in the elections between 1848 and 1852, which he treats as symptoms of "system tension," along with high levels of factional voting. See his "Partisanship and Ethnoreligious Conflict: The Third Electoral System, 1853–1892," in *The Evolution of American Electoral Systems*, ed. Kleppner et al., 116.

108. Polakoff, *Political Parties in American History*, 168.

109. See Thomas P. Slaughter, *Bloody Dawn: The Christiana Riot and Racial Violence in the Antebellum North* (New York: Oxford University Press, 1991).

110. Slaughter, *Bloody Dawn*, xi.

111. See Bruce Levine, "Conservatism, Nativism, and Slavery: Thomas R. Whitney and the Origins of the Know-Nothing Party," *The Journal of American History* 88, no. 2 (September 2001).

112. White, "Let My People Go," 1804–1860.

113. Holt, *The Rise and Fall of the American Whig Party*, 966.

114. Sundquist, *The Dynamics of the Party System*, 78. Sundquist is quoting Arthur Matthias Lee, "The Development of an Economic Policy in the Early Republican Party" (Ph.D. dissertation, Syracuse University, 1953), 23, 24, 44. Kleppner thinks that antislavery merely became the symbol for the cluster of moral issues associated with the evangelical revivalism: "Abolitionism turned antislavery, unleashed temperance and sabbatarian enthusiasm, resurgent antipopery, and pervasive antipartyism—all bound together symbolically in a broad antisouthernism—convulsed the political universe and ultimately coalesced to transform it." See Kleppner, *The Third Electoral System*, 62.

115. Sundquist, *Dynamics of the Party System*, 74–78.

116. Polakoff, *Political Parties in American History*, 178. Barrington Moore argues, however, that the new Republican Party rested on a bargain between business and farmers in the North, with business getting a higher tariff in exchange for support for the farmers' demand for land (130).

117. Polakoff, *Political Parties in American History*, 178–79.

118. Sundquist, *Dynamics of the Party System*, 70–71.

119. Polakoff, *Political Parties in American History*, 179.

120. See Nathan Newman and J. J. Gass, "A New Birth of Freedom: The Forgotten History of the 13th, 14th, and 15th Amendments," Judicial Independence Series (New York: Brennan Center for Justice at New York University School of Law, 2004), 7–8.

121. Polakoff, *Political Parties in American History*, 186–89.

122. Polakoff, *Political Parties in American History*, 189–90.

123. Polakoff, *Political Parties in American History*, 196–97.

124. See Eric Foner, "The Second American Revolution," in *The United States Constitution*, ed. Bertell Ollman and Jonathan Birnbaum (New York: New York University Press, 1990), 202.

125. See Franklin, *From Slavery to Freedom*, 279–83. Many slaves in the border states were unaffected by the Proclamation, and many in the rebel states did not hear about it. They had to wait for the Thirteenth Amendment, passed in 1865.

126. See Newman and Gass, *A New Birth of Freedom*, for an illuminating discussion of this period, which they call "A New Birth of Freedom."

Chapter Five

1. See Frances Fox Piven and Richard A. Cloward, *Regulating the Poor: The Functions of Public Welfare* (New York: Pantheon Books, 1971, updated 1993); *Poor People's Movements: How They Succeed, How They Fail* (New York: Pantheon Books, 1977); *The New Class War: Reagan's Attack on the Welfare State and Its Consequences* (New York: Pantheon Books, 1982); The *Breaking of the American Social Compact* (New York: New Press, 1997).

2. Charles Tilly, Louise Tilly, and Richard Tilly, *The Rebellious Century, 1830-1930* (Cambridge, MA: Harvard University Press, 1975), 290.

3. Charles Tilly, "Social Movements and National Politics," in *Statemaking and Social Movements*, ed. Charles Bright and Susan Harding (Ann Arbor: University of Michigan Press, 1984), 303.

4. Doug McAdam, John D. McCarthy, and Mayer Zald, "Social Movements," in *Handbook of Sociology*, ed. Neil Smelser (Beverly Hills, CA: Sage Publications, 1988), 727.

5. As to the wide agreement about the neglect of the study of the effects of social movements, see Marco G. Giugni, "Was It Worth the Effort? The Outcomes and Consequences of Social Movements," *Annual Review of Sociology* 24 (1998): 371–93.

6. Paul Burstein, Rachel L. Einwohner, and Jocelyn A. Hollander, "The Success of Political Movements: A Bargaining Perspective," in *The Politics of Social Protest: Comparative Perspectives on States and Social Movements*, ed. J. Craig Jenkins and Bert Klandersmans (Minneapolis: University of Minnesota Press, 1995), 276.

7. Edwin Amenta, Drew Halfmann, and Michael P. Young, "The Strategies and Contexts of Social Protest: Political Mediation and the Impact of the Townsend Movement in California," *Mobilization* 4, no. 1 (April 1999): 1.

8. Generalizations are always hazardous, and there are important exceptions to this one, particularly in the work of Gamson, Tarrow, and Gurr, who do try to assess movement outcomes. See William A. Gamson, *The Strategy of Social Protest* (Homewood, IL: Dorsey Press, 1975), as well as Jack A. Goldstone's critique of William A. Gamson, "The Weakness of Organization," *American Journal of Sociology* 85 (1980): 1017–42; and Sidney Tarrow, *Power in Movement: Social Movements, Collective Action and Politics* (New York: Cambridge University Press, 1994), chap. 9; Ted Robert Gurr, "On the Outcomes of Violent Conflict," in *The Handbook of Political Conflict*, ed. Ted Robert Gurr (New York: The Free Press, 1980), 238–94. Empirical studies of the civil rights movement also attempt to draw conclusions about outcomes, although analyses of the detailed mechanisms through which protests contributed to legislated outcomes are generally lacking. Nevertheless, I think my generalization stands as a characterization of the bulk of movement studies. Most recently,

see Kenneth T. Andrews, "The Impacts of Social Movements on the Political Process: The Civil Rights Movement and Black Electoral Politics in Mississippi," *American Sociological Review* 62 (October 1997); and Kenneth T. Andrews, "Contending Theories of Movement Outcomes" (paper presented at the Social Movements and Society Conference, University of California at Davis, August 20, 1998). See the work of Edwin Amenta and his colleagues on the impact of the Townsend movement on social security legislation. And later in this chapter I discuss the work of J. Craig Jenkins and Barbara Brents, which specifically discusses the impact of movements on Social Security legislation.

9. Marco Giugni, Edwin Amenta, and Michael Young discuss the conceptual difficulties studying the outcomes of collective challenges. See Marco Guigni, "Introduction: How Movements Matter: Past Research, Present Problems, Future Developments," and Edwin Amenta and Michael P. Young, "Making an Impact: Conceptual and Methodological Implications of the Collective Goods Criterion," in *How Social Movements Matter*, ed. Marco Guigni, Doug McAdam, and Charles Tilly (Minneapolis: University of Minnesota Press, 1999), 22–41.

10. Some analysts argue, however, that populist demands, defeated at the time, had longer term influence on the national policy agenda. See Elizabeth Sanders, *Roots of Reform: Farmers, Workers, and the American State, 1877-1917* (Chicago: University of Chicago Press, 1999); David Sarasohn, *The Party of Reform: Democrats in the Progressive Era* (Jackson: University Press of Mississippi, 1989).

11. See Robert V. Bruce, *1877: Year of Violence* (Chicago: University of Chicago Press, 1987).

12. See James Weinstein, *The Long Detour: The History and Future of the American Left* (Boulder, CO: Westview, 2004), chap. 2.

13. See Sanders, *Roots of Reform*, 31.

14. Sanders, *Roots of Reform*, chap. 3.

15. See Kevin Phillips, *Arrogant Capital* (Boston: Little, Brown and Company, 1994), 14.

16. On this point, see Kevin Phillips, *Wealth and Democracy: A Political History of the American Rich* (New York: Broadway Books, 2002), 236–44.

17. Phillips, *Wealth and Democracy*.

18. On the concentration of progressive reform in these periods, see Alexander Hicks, "Back to the Future? A review essay on income concentration and conservatism," *Socio-Economic Review* 1 (2003): 271–88.

19. See Frances Fox Piven and Richard A. Cloward, *Regulating the Poor: The Functions of Public Welfare* (New York: Vintage Books, 1993), chap. 3.

20. See James T. Patterson, *America's Struggle Against Poverty: 1900-1980* (Cambridge, MA: Harvard University Press, 1981), 57.

21. See Edwin Amenta, *Bold Relief: Institutional Politics and the Origins of American Social Policy* (Princeton, NJ: Princeton University Press, 1998), 5, 77. Amenta claims that the United States actually outspent any European power. Swenson takes issue with Amenta, however, claiming that Sweden actually surpassed the United States modestly in social spending, 8.5 percent of GDP compared to 6.3 percent for the United States, when spending by all levels of government is considered. See Peter A. Swenson, "Varieties of Capitalist Interests: Power, Institutions, and the Regulatory Welfare State in the United States and Sweden," *Studies in American Political Development* 18, no. 1 (Summer 2004): 1n3.

22. Statistics from the U. S. Department of Agriculture are compiled in Kenneth Finegold, "Agriculture and the Politics of U.S. Social Provision: Social Insurance and Food Stamps," in *The Politics of Social Policy in the United States*, ed. Margaret Weir, Ann Shola Orloff, and Theda Skocpol (Princeton, NJ: Princeton University Press, 1984), 223.

23. See Alice O'Connor, *Poverty Knowledge: Social Science, Social Policy, and the Poor in Twentieth-Century U.S. History* (Princeton, NJ: Princeton University Press, 2001), 240.

24. Frances Fox Piven and Richard A. Cloward, *The New Class War* (New York: Pantheon Books, 1985), 14–19.

25. This is not to deny that the National Labor Relations Act and the system of labor rights it established eventually failed workers. For a discussion, see David Brody, "Labor vs. the Law: How the Wagner Act Became a Management Tool," *New Labor Forum*, Spring 2004, 9–16; and Katherine Sciacchitano, "Labor Summit: Some Reactions and Observations," *Social Policy* 34, no. 1 (Fall 2003): 7–10.

26. David Plotke, "The Wagner Act, Again: Politics and Labor, 1935-37," *Studies in American Political Development* 3 (1989): 110.

27. For a compelling account of what unions were able to achieve in the post–World War II years, see Jack Metzgar, *Striking Steel: Solidarity Remembered* (Philadelphia: Temple University Press, 2000).

28. Irving Bernstein, *The Lean Years: A History of the American Worker, 1920-1933* (Baltimore, MD: Penguin Books, 1970), 421-23.

29. See Frances Fox Piven and Richard A. Cloward, *Poor People's Movements: How They Succeed, How They Fail* (New York: Pantheaon Books, 1977), chap. 2 and 3.

30. A survey in New York City revealed, for example, that almost all of the district relief offices reported frequent dealing with disruptive unemployed groups. See Alice Brophy and George Hallowitz, "Pressure Groups and the Relief Administration in New York City" (unpublished professional project, New York: New York School of Social Work, April 7, 1937).

31. U.S.Bureau of Labor Statistics, "Industrial Strikes and Strike Wave Index, 1936-55," cited in J. Craig Jenkins and Barbara G. Brents, "Social Protest, Hegemonic Competition, and Social Reform: A Political Struggle Interpretation of the Origins of the American Welfare State," *American Sociological Review* 54, no. 6 (1989): 891–907.

32. Piven and Cloward, *Poor People's Movements*, 126.

33. Bureau of the Census, *Historical Statistics*, D 970-985, "Work Stoppages, Workers Involved, Man-Days Idle, Major Issues, and Average Duration: 1881-1970."

34. See Paul Cammack, "Review Article: Bringing the State Back In?" *British Journal of Political Science* 19:261–90.

35. I draw in this critique particularly on Weir, Orloff, and Skocpol, *The Politics of Social Policy in the United States*; Amenta, *Bold Relief*; Ann Shola Orloff, *The Politics of Pensions* (Madison: University of Wisconsin Press, 1993); Theda Skocpol, *Protecting Mothers and Soldiers* (Cambridge, MA: Harvard University Press, 1992); Margaret Weir, *Politics and Jobs* (Princeton, NJ: Princeton University Press, 1992). See also Sven Steinmo, Kathleen Thelen, and Frank Longstreth, eds., *Structuring Politics: Historical Institutionalism in Comparative Analysis* (Cambridge: Cambridge University Press, 1992); Paul Pierson, *Dismantling the Welfare State? Reagan, Thatcher, and the Politics of Retrenchment* (Cambridge: Cambridge University Press, 1994); P. Evans, D. Rueschemeyer, and T. Skocpol, eds., *Bringing the State Back In* (Cambridge: Cambridge University Press, 1985); Peter A. Hall and Rosemary C. R. Taylor, "Political Science and the Three New Institutionalisms," *Political Studies*, 44 (1996): 936–971.

36. The comparison deserves to be made with more caution than I exercise here. The United States did remain well behind some European powers—England and Belgium, for example—in the extent of industrialization. But it was ahead of other nations, such as Sweden and Norway, that initiated welfare programs early. The cross-national comparison of the development of democratic rights is also complicated, since the early-nineteenth-century expansion of the male franchise in the United States was followed half a century later by the introduction of drastic legal and procedural limits on the right to vote. See Frances Fox Piven and Richard A. Cloward, *Why Americans Don't Vote* (New York: Pantheon, 1988).

37. Margaret Weir, Ann Shola Orloff, and Theda Skocpol, "Introduction: Understanding American Social Politics," in *The Politics of Social Policy in the United States*, ed. Weir, Orloff, and Skocpol, 9.

38. Edwin Amenta and Theda Skocpol, "Redefining the New Deal: World War II and the Development of Social Provision in the United States," in *The Politics of Social Policy in the United States*, ed. Weir, Orloff, and Skocpol. Similarly, Weir in *Politics and Jobs: The Boundaries of Employment Policy in the United States* (Princeton, NJ: Princeton University Press, 1992), 167, argues with regard to

employment policy that "sequences of policy and institutional creation bounded later policymaking."

39. Weir, *Politics and Jobs*, 24.

40. Karen Orren and Stephen Skowronek, *The Search for American Political Development* (Cambridge: Cambridge University Press, 2004), 101.

41. Jacob Hacker and Paul Pierson also offer a broadly institutionalist argument in explaining the social policy initiatives of the 1930s. However, they focus not on political and policy institutions, but on economic institutions, and argue that the consequence of economic collapse was to weaken both the structural and instrumental power of business, allowing popular political claimants to exert more influence. See "Business Power and Social Policy: Employers and the Formation of the American Welfare State," *Politics & Society* 30, no. 2 (June 2002): 277–325. For the argument that the institutionalists fasten on the wrong institutions in accounting for policy change, see Frances Fox Piven, "The Politics of Retrenchment: The U.S. Case," in *Oxford Handbook on Social Welfare*, 1621–1653.

42. Patterson, *America's Struggle against Poverty*, 58.

43. See Colin Gordon, "New Deal, Old Deck: Business and the Origins of Social Security, 1920-1935," *Politics and Society* 19, no. 2 (June, 1991): 165–207. Gordon treats corporate welfare programs as more important than state precedents, but these are beyond the purview of historical-institutionalists.

44. Weir, *Politics and Jobs*, 75–78.

45. See Frances Fox Piven, "The Great Society as Political Strategy," *The Columbia Forum* 13, no. 2 (Summer 1970).

46. Thus Orloff first agrees that social movements were "of critical importance" to New Deal initiatives, but then disposes of their role by asserting that certainly "it is not the case that the Social Security Act was a direct product of mass movements," as if, in a complicated world, anything is simply a direct product of anything else. See Ann Shola Orloff, "The Political Origins of America's Belated Welfare State," in *The Politics of Social Policy in the United States*, ed. Weir, Orloff, and Skocpol, 66.

47. See Theda Skocpol and John Ikenberry, "The Political Formation of the American Welfare State in Historical and Comparative Perspective," in *Comparative Social Research*, ed. Richard F. Tomasson (Greenwhich, CT: JAI Press, 1983).

48. See Theda Skocpol, "Political Response to Capitalist Crisis: Neo-Marxist Theories of the State and the Case of the New Deal, *Politics and Society* 10, no. 2 (1980): 155–201.

49. See Theda Skocpol, "The Limits of the New Deal System and the Roots of Contemporary Welfare Dilemmas," in *The Politics of Social Policy in the United States*, ed. Weir, Orloff, and Skocpol, 304–305.

50. See Weir, *Politics and Jobs*, 83–89. Weir also includes social movements in a list of events that are essentially exogenous to politics, such as economic change or international political developments (25).

51. Adam D. Sheingate, "Political Entrepreneurship, Institutional Change, and American Political Development," *Studies in American Political Development* 17, no. 2 (Fall 2003): 185.

52. For discussions of social welfare reformers, see for example Robert Bremmer, *Up From the Depths: The Discovery of Poverty in the United States* (New York: New York University Press, 1956); Michael B. Katz, *In the Shadow of the Poor House* (New York: Basic Books, 1986); Walter Trattner, *From Poor Law to Welfare State* (New York: Free Press, 1979). Andrew Achenbaum, writing about the social policies of the 1930s, inventories the evidence that needs to be considered to establish the influence of reformers, including "the writings and published speeches of religious figures, philanthropists, and social reformers" and "public documents, including congressional hearings and debates; court decisions at the local, state, and federal levels; as well as the proceedings and annual reports of municipal and state public welfare bodies." See Andrew W. Achenbaum, "The Formative Years of Social Security: A Test of the Piven and Cloward Thesis," in *Social Welfare or Social Control: Some Historical Reflections on "Regulating the Poor,"* ed. Walter I. Trattner (Knoxville: University of Tennessee Press, 1983).

53. See Skocpol, *Protecting Mothers and Soldiers*. We should note that Skocpol here departs from her earlier characterization of the United States as a social policy laggard until the first "big bang" of the 1930s and instead argues that the maternalist programs promoted by women reformers made the United States a social policy pioneer.

54. See David Plotke, *Building a Democratic Political Order: Reshaping American Liberalism in the 1930s and 1940s* (Cambridge: Cambridge University Press, 1996), 112. Unlike many other analysts who emphasize the role of reformers, Plotke posits a more complex causality. Working class political action was "significant," but the upsurge itself did not dictate the response.

55. See David Plotke, "The Wagner Act, Again: Politics and Labor, 1935-37," in *Studies in American Political Development*, v. 3 (New Haven, CT: Yale University Press, 1989), 105–56.

56. See Patterson, *America's Struggle against Poverty*, chap. 4.

57. Heclo, who set a precedent for this depiction of state actors as reformers, depicts civil servants as reformers, motivated by moral and policy ideas, in the development of the British and Swedish welfare state. See Hugh Heclo, *Modern Social Politics in Britain and Sweden* (New Haven, CT: Yale University Press, 1974).

58. Theda Skocpol and G. John Ikenberry, "The Political Formation of the American Welfare State in Historical and Comparative Perspective," *Comparative Social Research* 6 (1983): 87–148.

59. See Daniel Patrick Moynihan, *Maximum Feasible Misunderstanding: Community Action in the War on Poverty* (New York: Free Press, 1969).

60. See for example Weir, *Politics and Jobs*, 69–75.

61. See Weir, *Politics and Jobs*, 63, 69. See also Margaret Weir, Ann Shola Orloff, and Theda Skocpol, who similarly blame a "national network of poverty researchers" for the emphasis on poverty instead of labor markets, in "Epilogue: The Future of Social Policy in the United States: Political Constraints and Possibilities," in *The Politics of Social Policy in the United States*, ed. Weir, Orloff, and Skocpol, 424–25.

62. Alice O'Connor, *Poverty Knowledge: Social Science, Social Policy, and the Poor in Twentieth-Century U.S. History* (Princeton, NJ: Princeton University Press, 2001), 140–65.

63. See William A. Gamson, *Strategy of Social Protest* (Homewood, IL: Dorsey Press, 1975), 112–17. Twenty of the total sample of organizations were occupationally based, many of them unions; seventeen were reform groups, including for example the American Anti-Slavery Society, A. Philip Randolph's March on Washington Committee, the International Workingmen's Association, and a variety of third parties.

64. For examples of power elite theorists in addition to those discussed below, see G. William Domhoff, *The Power Elite and the State* (New York: Aldine De Gruyter, 1990); Thomas Ferguson, "From Normalcy to New Deal: Industrial Structure, Party Competition, and American Public Policy in the Great Depression," *International Organization* 38, no. 1 (1984): 41–94; and Jill Quadagno, "Welfare Capitalism and the Social Security Act of 1935," *American Sociological Review* 49 (1984): 632–36. There are of course differences among these analysts, some having to do with underlying conceptions of class, class fractions, and class politics, and others having to do with the empirical patterns of elite coalescence and division with regard to twentieth-century policy initiatives. For more theoretical neo-Marxist analyses, see Ralph Miliband, *The State in Capitalist Society*, (London, Quartet Books, 1973); Nicos Poulantzas, *Political Power and Social Classes* (London: Verso, 1968); and James O'Connor, *The Fiscal Crisis of the State* (New York: St. Martin's Press, 1973). For examples of work which fastens on "corporate liberalism," as the generator of reform, see Martin J. Sklar, *The Corporate Reconstruction of American Capitalism, 1890-1916: The Market, The Law, and Politics* (Cambridge: Cambridge University Press, 1988); James Weinstein, *The Corporate Ideal in the Liberal State: 1900-1918* (Boston: Beacon Press, 1968); James Livingston,

Origins of the Federal Reserve System: Money, Class and Corporate Capitalism, 1890-1913 (Ithaca, NY: Cornel University Press, 1986); and Gabriel Kolko, *The Triumph of Conservatism* (New York: Free Press, 1977).

65. See, for example, Samuel P. Hays, *Conservation and the Gospel of Efficiency* (Cambridge, MA: Harvard University Press, 1958); and Weinstein, *The Corporate Ideal*.

66. See Skocpol and Ikenberry, "The Political Formation of the American Welfare State."

67. See Domhoff, *The Power Elite and the State*, 44–52; and also by G. William Domhoff, *State Autonomy or Class Domiance? Case Studies on Policy-Making in America* (New York: Aldine de Gruyter, 1996), 117–76.

68. See Colin Gordon, "New Deal, Old Deck: Business and the Origins of Social Security, 1920-1935," *Politics and Society* 19, no. 2 (June 1991); Peter A. Swenson, *Capitalists against Markets* (New York: Oxford University Press, 2002); and also by Swenson, "Varieties of Capitalist Interests: Power, Institutions, and the Regulatory Welfare State in the United States and Sweden," *Studies in American Political Development* 18, no. 1 (Spring 2004): 1–29.

69. Gordon here quotes the Special Conference Committee, a secretive organization of business executives. Colin Gordon, "New Deal, Old Deck," 168.

70. Gordon, "New Deal, Old Deck," 179.

71. U.S. Senate, Committee on Finance, *Economic Security Act: Hearings on S. 1130* (Washington, DC: U.S. Government Printing Office, 1935), 284, quoted in Swenson, "Varieties of Capitalist Interest," 7.

72. Swenson, *Capitalists against Markets*, 41.

73. See Quadagno, "Welfare Capitalism and the Social Security Act of 1935," 1984.

74. See Ferguson, "From Normalcy to New Deal," esp. 47–61.

75. See Domhoff, *The Power Elite and the State*, esp. chap. 4.

76. Gordon, "New Deal, Old Deck," 191.

77. Swenson hedges about Social Security, however. As for social security he notes, "Actual pressure for reform came from other social groups mobilized on mass basis in elections and other modes of direct political participation." Swenson, *Capitalists against Markets*.

78. Jacob S. Hacker and Paul Pierson, "Varieties of Capitalist Interests and Capitalist Power: A Response to Swenson," *Studies in American Political Development* 18, no. 2 (Fall 2004), 188–89.

79. Phillips, *Arrogant Capital*, 16–17.

80. Kristi Andersen, *The Creation of a Democratic Majority, 1928-1936* (Chicago: University of Chicago Press, 1979). See also Angus Campbell, Philip Converse,

Walter Miller, and Donald Stokes, *The American Voter* (New York: John Wiley, 1960); Carl Degler, "American Political Parties and the Rise of the City: An Interpretation," *Journal of America History* 51 (June 1964): 41–59; Samuel Lubell, *The Future of American Politics* (New York: Harper, 1951).

81. V. O. Key, "A Theory of Critical Elections," *Journal of Politics* 17 (1955).

82. James L. Sundquist, *Dynamics of the Party System* (Washington, DC: The Brookings Institution, 1973), chap. 10.

83. Walter Dean Burnham, *Critical Elections and the Mainsprings of American Politics* (New York: W. W. Norton and Company, 1970), esp. chap. 5.

84. Burnham, *Critical Elections*, 10.

85. See Benjamin Ginsberg, "Elections and Public Policy," *American Political Science Review* 70, no. 1 (March 1976): 41–49.

86. Richard Bensel, *Sectionalism and American Political Development, 1880-1980* (Madison: University of Wisconsin Press, 1984), chap. 4.

87. V. O. Key, *The Responsible Electorate: Rationality in Presidential Voting, 1936-1960* (New York: Vintage Books, 1968), esp. chap. 3, provides one of the earliest expositions of the argument.

88. Sundquist, *Dynamics of the Party System*, does discuss the distinctive role of party "zealots," however. And Schattschneider, while he has nothing to say about twentieth-century social movements, gives a large role to the populist movement in precipitating the sectional realignment of 1896. See E. E. Schattschneider, *The Semisovereign People: A Realist's View of Democracy in America* (New York: Holt, Rinehart and Winston, 1960), 78–82.

89. V. O. Key, *The Responsible Electorate*, 7–8.

90. See Plotke, "The Wagner Act, Again," 140.

91. J. Craig Jenkins and Barbara G. Brents, "Social Protest, Hegemonic Competition, and Social Reform: A Political Struggle Interpretation of the Origins of the American Welfare State," *American Sociological Review* 54 (1989): 891–909.

92. See Jenkins and Brents, "Social Protest," 896–97.

93. See for example Robert B. Albritton, "Social Amelioration Through Mass Insurgency? A Reexamination of the Piven and Cloward Thesis," *American Political Science Review* 73 (December 1979).

94. For a discussion, see Piven and Cloward, *Poor People's Movements*; and Frances Fox Piven and Richard A. Cloward, "Movements and Dissensus Politics," in *The Breaking of the American Social Compact*, ed. Piven and Cloward (New York: New Press, 1997).

95. On the influence of activists on the Democratic Party, see Thomas B. Edsall, *The New Politics of Inequality* (New York: W. W. Norton, 1984). For a more general discussion that attributes a large role to party activists in generating more

polarized party agendas, see John H. Aldrich, *Why Parties?* (Chicago: University of Chicago Press, 1995). Aldrich thinks this development has created a new type of political party. We think it is more likely the transient result of the rise of movements, first on the left, and then on the right.

96. On the polarization of party appeals during realigning periods, see Ginsberg, "Elections and Public Policy," 43, table 1.

Chapter Six

1. See Frances Fox Piven and Richard A. Cloward, *Poor People's Movements: Why They Succeed, How They Fail* (New York: Pantheon Books, 1977), chap. 1.

2. However, until the election of 1828 and the development of the mass party system discussed in chapter 4, the turnout pattern remained volatile. For a discussion, see Frances Fox Piven and Richard A. Cloward, *Why Americans Still Don't Vote* (Boston: Beacon Press, 2000), chap. 3.

3. Richard McCormick, "Political Development and the Second Party System," in *The American Party Systems: Stages of Political Development*, ed. William Nisbet Chambers and Walter Dean Burnham (New York: Oxford University Press, 1967), 108.

4. Alexis de Tocqueville, *Democracy in America* (1838; repr., New York: Anchor Books, 1969), 242–43.

5. On this point, see Paul Kleppner, *The Third Electoral System: Parties, Voters and Political Cultures* (Chapel Hill: University of North Carolina Press, 1979); and also by Kleppner, "Partisanship and Ethnoreligious Conflict: The Third Electoral System, 1853-1892," in *The Evolution of American Electoral Systems*, ed. Paul Kleppner et al. (Westport, CT: Greenwood Press, 1981).

6. de Tocqueville, *Democracy in America*, 242–43.

7. On this point, see S. N. Eisenstadt and Luis Roniger, "The Study of Patron-Client Relations and Recent Development in Sociological Theory," and Rene Lemarchand, "Comparative Political Clientelism: Structure, Process, and Optic," both in *Political Clientelism, Patronage and Development*, ed. S. N. Eisenstadt and Rene Lemarchand (Beverly Hills, CA: Sage Publications, 1981). See also Nicos Mouzelis, "On the Concept of Populism: Populist and Clientelist Modes of Incorporation in Semiperipheral Politics," in *Politics and Society* 14, no. 3 (1985).

8. John Hope Franklin, *From Slavery to Freedom: A History of Negro Americans* (New York: Vintage, 1969), 303.

9. See Nathan Newman and J. J. Gass, *A New Birth of Freedom: The Forgotten History of the 13th, 14th, and 15th Amendments*, Judicial Independence Series (New York: Brennan Center for Justice at the New York University School of Law,

2004), 11. See also Eric Foner, *Reconstruction: America's Unfinished Revolution, 1863-1877* (New York: Harper and Row, 1988); and C. Vann Woodward, *Origins of the New South, 1877-1913* (Baton Rouge: Louisiana State University Press, 1951).

10. Newman and Gass, *A New Birth of Freedom*, 12,14.

11. Kleppner, *The Third Electoral System*, 93.

12. The enforcement provisions of the legislation were modeled on the Fugitive Slave Act of 1850, and criminalized violations of civil rights by private persons and authorized stiff fines for those violations. See Newman and Gass, *A New Birth of Freedom*, 11. Congress also banned segregation in private institutions, and this a century before the civil rights movement (2).

13. Newman and Gass, *A New Birth of Freedom*, 14–15.

14. See Woodward, *Origins of the New South*, 179; Franklin, *From Slavery to Freedom*, 322–23.

15. The title of the Newman and Gass work

16. Vann Woodward reports, for example, that every session of the Virginia General Assembly between 1869 and 1891 contained black members. In North Carolina, fifty-two blacks were elected to the lower house of the state legislature between 1876 and 1894, and between 1878 and 1902, forty-seven blacks served in the South Carolina General Assembly. As late as 1890 there were still sixteen black members in the session of the Louisiana General Assembly that passed the bill in 1890 requiring segregation on the railroads and leading to the *Plessy v. Ferguson* ruling by the Supreme Court. See C. Vann Woodward, *The Strange Career of Jim Crow* (New York: Galaxy Press, 1964), 54.

17. Under the lien system, the farmer pledged his future crop to merchants, who were often also large landowners, in return for supplies and credit. Farmers were also hostage to merchants who sold their crops and determined the prices they received. These arrangements drove farmers to rely more on cotton agriculture, although cotton prices, along with other agricultural prices, were in free fall in the decades after the Civil War. See Woodward, *Origins of the New South*, chap. 7.

18. See Desmond S. King and Rogers M. Smith, "Racial Orders in American Political Development," *American Political Science Review* 99, no. 1 (February 2005): 75–92.

19. For an overview, see Morgan J. Kousser, *The Shaping of Southern Politics: Suffrage Restriction and the Establishment of the One-Party South, 1880-1910* (New Haven, CT: Yale University Press, 1974).

20. See Frances Fox Piven and Richard A. Cloward, *Why Americans Still Don't Vote, And Why Politicians Want It That Way* (Boston: Beacon Press, 2000), chap. 4. On felon disenfranchisement and its relation to the "Menace of Negro Domination," see Angela Behrens, Christopher Uggen, and Jeff Manza, "Ballot Manipulation and

the 'Menace of Negro Domination': Racial Threat and Felon Disenfranchisement in the United States, 1850-2002," *American Journal of Sociology* 109, no. 3 (November 2003), 559–605.

21. See Woodward, *The Strange Career of Jim Crow*, 82, passim.

22. King and Rogers, "Racial Orders in American Political Development," 1.

23. See Piven and Cloward, *Poor People's Movements*, 145–46.

24. Irving Bernstein, *Turbulent years: A History of the American Worker, 1933-41* (Boston: Houghton Mifflin Co., 1971), 468.

25. Piven and Cloward, *Poor People's Movements*, 153–55.

26. Michael Goldfield reports on union membership growth in the United States and its subsequent decline, and compares these numbers to other Western countries. See Michael Goldfield, *The Decline of Organized Labor in the United States* (Chicago: University of Chicago Press, 1987), chap. 1.

27. Jack Metzgar, *Striking Steel: Solidarity Remembered* (Philadelphia: Temple University Press, 2000), 37–38.

28. Cited in David Bacon, "Change Direction or Die," truthout/perspective, www.truthout.org/docs_2005/L022105H.shtml.

29. See Nelson Lichtenstein, *Walter Ruether the Most Dangerous Man in Detroit* (Urbana: University of Illinois Press, 1995); Stanley Aronowitz, "On the Future of American Labor," *Working USA: The Journal of Labor and Society* 8, no. 3 (March 2005): 271–91.

30. In 1937, the Supreme Court ruled that sit-down workers could be fired.

31. Piven and Cloward, *Poor People's Movements*, 157.

32. Philip Taft and Philip Ross, "American Labor Violence: Its Causes, Character, and Outcome," in *The History of Violence in America: A Report to the National Commission on the Causes and Prevention of Violence*, ed. Hugh Davis Graham and Ted Robert Gurr (New York: Praeger Publishers, 1969), 378–79.

33. Metzgar, *Striking Steel*, 36. On this point, see also David Brody, "Workplace Contractualism: A Historical/Comparative Analysis," in David Brody, *In Labor's Cause: Main Themes on the History of the American Worker* (New York: Oxford University Press, 1993).

34. Metzgar, *Striking Steel*, 55. Metzgar goes on to say that his steelworker father, a grievance officer for the union, viewed the bureaucratic apparatus that resulted from the new regime as a way of slowly eroding management authority.

35. See Mike Davis, *Prisoners of the American Dream: Politics and Economy in the History of the U.S. Working Class* (London: Verso, 1986).

36. "[L]abor's political power decreased after the 1930s," says Bill Winders, "because it 1) became clearly wedded to the Democratic Party and 2) aimed to control workers' potential of disrupting the economy. . . . When unions became

strongly wedded to the Democratic Party and to collective bargaining, labor lost some of its power." Bill Winders, "Maintaining the Coalition: Class Coalitions and Policy Trajectories," *Politics and Society* 33, no. 3 (September 2005): 1–37.

37. See Arthur M. Schlesinger Jr., *The Age of Roosevelt*, vol. 3, *The Politics of Upheaval, 1935-1938* (Boston: Houghton Mifflin Co., 1960); Davis J. Greenstone, *Labor in American Politics* (New York: Vintage Books, 1969).

38. Metzgar, *Striking Steel*, 90–91

39. See James J. Matles and James J. Higgins, *Them and Us: Struggles of a Rank-and-File Union* (Englewood Cliffs, NJ: Prentice-Hall, 1974), 118.

40. See David Swanson, "Strikes: Civil Contributions or Civil Disturbances?" truthout/perspective, www.truthout.org/docs_2005/L021505A.shtml.

41. According to Harry Millis, a University of Chicago economist involved in the writing of the National Labor Relations Act, by the mid-1940s, the board was "leaning over backward to be fair to employers" by failing to enforce the labor protections in the act. See Harry Millis and E. C. Brown, *From the Wagner Act to Taft-Hartley* (Chicago: University of Chicago Press, 1950).

42. Metzgar, *Striking Steel*, 54.

43. Metzgar, *Striking Steel*, 225–27.

44. Greg Ip, "As Economy Shifts, A New Generation Fights to Keep Up, *Wall Street Journal*, June 22, 2005.

45. For discussions of declining Democratic strength over the course of the postwar period, see Martin P. Wattenberg, *The Decline of American Political Parties* (Cambridge, MA: Harvard University Press). See also David Plotke, who shows that the argument that attributes the party's troubles to changes in the party's convention rules is wrong. See "Party Reform as Failed Democratic Renewal in the United States," *Studies in American Political Development* 10, no. 2 (Fall 1996): 223–88.

46. For an extended discussion of the role of the Democratic Party in promoting deindustrialization, see Frances Fox Piven, "Structural Constraints and Political Development: The Case of the American Democratic Party," in *Labor Parties in Postindustrial Societies*, ed. Frances Fox Piven (Cambridge: Polity Press, 1991), 235–64.

47. Plotke calls this a "Democratic political order," but means essentially the same thing. "From the 1930s through the 1960s, it dominated American political life. By political order I mean a durable way of organizing and exercising political power at the national level. A political order includes distinct institutions, policies, and discourses, with durable links among them." See Plotke, "Party Reform and Democratic Renewal," 224.

48. Gallup data show that Democratic congressional voting among whites with "middle socioeconomic status" fell from 60 percent in 1960 to 49 percent in 1972.

Among whites with "low socioeconomic status" the decline was from 66 percent to 54 percent. Reported in Plotke, "Party Reform as Failed Democratic Renewal," 240n37.

49. Plotke, "Party Reform and Democratic Renewal," 250.

50. For a discussion, see Alexander Hicks, "Back to the Future? A Review Essay on Income Concentration and Conservatism," *Socio-Economic Review* no. 1 (2003), 271–88.

51. For a discussion, see Herbert J. Gans, "Race as Class," *Contexts*, November 2005. The median white household earned 62 percent more income, and possessed twelve times the wealth of the median black household. See Melvin Oliver and Thomas Shapiro, *Black Wealth/White Wealth: A New Perspective on Racial Inequality* (New York: Routledge, 1997), 86–90, 96–103.

52. The shift in public opinion is notable. In 1944, only 45 percent of Americans agreed that African Americans should have as good a chance as white people to get any kind of job. Three decades later, 97 percent agreed. Benjamin I. Page and Robert Y. Shapiro, *The Rational Public: Fifty Years of Trends in America's Policy Preferences* (Chicago: University of Chicago Press, 1992), 63; 68–71.

53. Edward R. Tufte initiated this interpretation with his argument that politicians standing for election tried to coordinate the business cycle with the election cycle. See *Political Control of the Economy* (Princeton, NJ: Princeton University Press, 1978).

54. Presidential Papers of Dwight D. Eisenhower, Document 1147, www .eisenhowermemorial.org/presidential-papers/first-term/documents/1147.cfm.

55. Hacker and Pierson argue that what is important about the Great Depression, is "the marked variation in business influence before, during, and after the New Deal. Prior to the Great Depression, business occupied a privileged position in American politics thanks to the structural power conferred upon it by the decentralized character of American federalism." But business lost some of this structural power when the locus of decision making shifted to the federal government. Moreover, business also lost instrumental power as a result of the widespread popular political mobilization. See Jacob S. Hacker and Paul Pierson, "Business Power and Social Policy," *Politics and Society* 30, no. 2 (June 2002), 277–325.

56. Pierre Bourdieu refers to this as a "veritable symbolic counterrevolution" that "seeks the restoration of the past order in some of its most archaic aspects (especially as regards economic relations)," yet it passes itself off as forward-looking. See Pierre Bourdieu, *Firing Back: Against the Tyranny of the Market* (New York: New Press, 2001), 24.

57. See Lewis Lapham, "Tentacles of Rage: The Republican propaganda mill, a brief history," *Harper's Magazine*, September 2004.

58. The targets of the campaign, in other words, were what Pierre Bourdieu calls "the left hand of the state, the set of agents of the so-called spending ministries which are the trace, within the state, of the social struggles of the past." See Pierre Bourdieu, *Acts of Resistance: Against the New Myths of Our Time* (New York: New Press, 1998), 2

59. For a discussion, see Robert Parry, "The Answer Is Fear," *The Progressive Populist* 11, no. 12 (July 1, 2005): 12.

60. See Ben H. Bagdikian, *The New Media Monopoly* (Boston: Beacon Press, 2004); and Lawrence Lessig, *Free Culture: How Big Media Uses Technology and the Law to Lock Down Culture and Control Creativity* (New York: Penguin, 2004).

61. See Joshua Chaffin, "America's Public Broadcasting Services Come under Siege," *Financial Times*, June 25–26, 2005, 7; Stephen Labaton "Official Had Aide Send Data to White House, *New York Times*, June 18, 2005, B7; Stephen Labaton and Anne E. Kornblut, "Ex-G.O.P. Official Become Public Broadcasting Chief," *New York Times*, June 24, 2005.

62. See Elizabeth Drew, "He's Back!" *New York Review*, March 5, 2005.

63. Linda Kintz, "God Goes Corporate," *New Labor Forum* 14, no. 1 (Spring 2005), 56.

64. The quote is from George Gilder, *Renewing American Civilization*, a textbook developed for a Newt Gingrich course. Cited in Kintz, "God Goes Corporate," 51.

65. Mike Gecan, "Taking Faith Seriously," *Boston Review*, April/May 2005.

66. The quotation is from a speech to the Commonwealth Club in 1932. See Aaron Singer, ed., *Campaign Speeches of American Presidential Candidates* (New York: Unger, 1976), cited in Ronald Schurin, "A Party Form of Government" (PhD dissertation completed at the Graduate School of the City University of New York, 1996). Schurin argues that this definition of the role of government was a strong and consistent theme in Roosevelt's public addresses.

67. This is from Stanley B. Greenberg's reminiscence, "How We Found—and Lost—a Majority," *The American Prospect*, June, 2005. Greenberg's 1991 article, "From Crisis to Working Majority," was considered a key guide for the Clinton 1992 campaign.

68. See Jonathan Schell's review of two Morris books, *The New Prince: Machiavelli Updated for the Twenty-first Century*, and *Behind the Oval Office: Getting Reelected Against All Odds*. Schell's review is "Master of All He Surveys," *The Nation*, June 21, 1999.

69. John Podesta, in an interview reported in the *New York Times* Magazine, asserts three goals of changes in tax policy: to eliminate taxation on wealth and investment; to reduce the size of government by reducing the revenue stream; and by shifting the tax burden to wages, to generate massive middle-class resistance to

tax rises. See Nicholas Confessore, "A Question of Numbers," *New York Times Magazine*, January 16, 2005, 38. See also William Greider, "Rolling Back the 20th Century," *Nation*, May 12, 2003.

70. Quoted by Paul Krugman, "Stating the Obvious," *New York Times*, May 27, 2003.

71. Kevin Phillips, *Wealth and Democracy: A Political History of the American Rich* (New York: Broadway Books, 2002), 422.

72. Christopher Swann, "Salaries Stagnate as Balance of Power Shifts to Employers," *Financial Times*, May 11, 2005.

73. Robert Pear, "States Proposing Sweeping Change to Trim Medicaid," *New York Times*, May 9, 2005.

74. See Sharon Parrott and John Springer, "Federal Budgets—Bad and Badde," ProgressiveTrail.org/articles/050406/ParrottandJohnSpringer.shtml?mail=06.

75. Robert Pear, "Bush Officials Spell Out Cuts in Money for Housing," *New York Times*, February 4, 2005.

76. In 1980, 30 million workers were covered by private defined-benefit pensions which supplemented their Social Security benefits. Only 14.4 million workers were covered by defined contribution plans, such as 401(k)s, subject to the vagaries of the market. By 1999, the numbers with defined benefit pensions had dropped by one quarter, while the number in defined contribution plans had exploded to 47 million. See Juan Gonzalez, "Labor's Future in the Imperial Age," *New Labor Forum* 14, no. 2 (Summer 2005), 32.

77. For a discussion see William Greider, "Riding Into the Sunset: Aging and how we'll pay for it," *The Nation*, June 27, 2005.

78. Steve Connor, "Global Warming Is 'Twice as Bad As Previously Thought,' " *The Independent U.K.*, January 27, 2005; Ian Bell, "Now Blair Can Lead the War on Environmental Chaos: So, Will He? Yes . . . When Texas Freezes Over," *The Sunday Herald*, January 30, 2005.

79. After falling to less than 8 percent at the end of World War II, the income share of the top 1 percent of income earners in the United States grew to 15 percent by the end of the century, while the share of the top 0.1 percent rose from 2 percent in 1978 to 6 percent in 1999. See G. Dumenil and D. Levy, "Neoliberal Dynamics: Toward a New Phase?" in *Managing Crises after the Imperial Turn*, ed. K. van der Pijl, L. Assassi, and D. Wigans (New York: Palgrave Macmillan, 2004), 41–63, cited and discussed in David Harvey, *A Brief History of Neoliberalism* (New York: Oxford, 2005), 15–17. Kevin Phillips reports that fully 60 percent of Americans saw a decline in their net worth. See Pillips, *Wealth and Democracy*, xviii and 396.

Epilogue

1. For a discussion and data on the correlation between income concentration and conservatism, see Alex Hicks, "Back to the Future? A Review Essay on Income Concentration and Conservatism," *Socio-Economic Review* 1 (2003): 271–88.

2. *State of Working America 2002/2003*, 16. The United States was the OECD leader in average annual hours at work. See Ken Estey, "Review of *Labor's Time: Shorter Hours, the UAW, and the Struggle for American Unionism*, by Jonathan Cutler," *WorkingUSA: The Journal of Labor and Society* 8, no. 3 (March 2005): 370–74.

3. See Robin Toner and Marjorie Connelly, "Bush's Support on Major Issues Tumbles in Poll," *New York Times*, June 17, 2005.

4. Colin Crouch, *Coping with Post-Democracy* (London: Fabian Society, 2000), 72.

5. Bob Master and Hetty Rosenstein, "Beyond Bureaucratic Restructuring: Mobilization and Politics Must Drive Labor's Revival from the Bottom Up," *Social Policy* 35, no. 3 (Spring 2005): 13.

6. Aronowitz points out that union density in an industry has not always produced victories, and points to the defeats suffered by the UAW in the farm equipment industry where density was very high. See Stanley Aronowitz, "On the Future of American Labor," *WorkingUSA: The Journal of Labor and Society* 8, no. 3 (March 2005): 271–91.

7. See Mark Dudzic, "Saving the Right to Organize: Substituting the Thirteenth Amendment for the Wagner Act," *New Labor Forum* 14, no. 1 (Spring 2005): 60.

8. Personal communication, June 25, 2005.

9. See the discussion in Frances Fox Piven and Richard A. Cloward, *Poor People's Movements: Why They Succeed, How They Fail* (New York: Pantheon Books, 1977), chap. 3.

10. Jack Metzgar, "Is This The Second Coming of the CIO?" *New Labor Forum* 14, no. 2 (Summer 2005): 17.

11. Dudzic reports, on the basis of Bureau of Labor Statistics data, that "the number of workers on strike has experienced a seven-fold decline between 1974 and 2001. During that same period, average inflation adjusted wages have declined by over eight percent." See Mark Dudzic, "Saving the Right to Organize," 60.

12. Edna Bonacich and Jake B. Wilson, "Hoisted by Its Own Petard: Organizing Wal-Mart's Logistic Workers," *New Labor Forum* 14, no. 2 (Summer 2005): 74.

Index

About the Author

❧

FRANCES FOX PIVEN is the distinguished professor of political science and sociology at the Graduate School at the City University of New York and president of the American Sociological Association. She is the author or coauthor of fourteen books, most recently *The War at Home: The Domestic Costs of Bush's Militarism* and *Why Americans Still Don't Vote: And Why Politicians Want It That Way*. She coauthored with Richard Cloward *Regulating the Poor* and *Poor People's Movements*. She lives in Manhattan and Millerton, New York.

Breinigsville, PA USA
11 October 2010
247136BV00002B/3/P

9 780742 563162